CANAPES

CANAPES

Eric Treuille and Victoria Blashford-Snell

PHOTOGRAPHY BY IAN O'LEARY

A Dorling Kindersley Book

A Dorling Kindersley Book

New Edition
EDITORS Shannon Beatty, Penny Warren
MANAGING EDITOR Stephanie Farrow
SENIOR ART EDITOR Rosamund Saunders
DTP DESIGNER Sonia Charbonnier

Original Edition
EDITORIAL CONSULTANT Rosie Kindersley
DESIGN AND ART DIRECTION Stuart Jackman
PROJECT EDITOR Julia Pemberton Hellums
ASSISTANT EDITOR Sally Somers
EDITORIAL ASSISTANT Phil Poyer
PRODUCTION CONTROLLER Elizabeth Cherry

FOOD STYLING Eric Treuille

DEDICATION
To my wife.
To my husband.

First published in Great Britain in 1999 by
Dorling Kindersley Limited,
80 Strand, London WC2R 0RL

ISBN-13: 978-1-4053-0513-6

CONTENTS

INTRODUCTION

From the simplest to the grandest party, entertaining means sharing. Since time immemorial, the traditional way to express friendship has been with an open house, a warm welcome and good food lovingly prepared. We were fortunate enough to grow up in households where home-cooked meals were a pleasurable ritual that punctuated our lives. Then, we learnt the joy of connecting with family and friends over food. Now, many people don't seem to have the time or the energy to cook, let alone entertain, at home. The constraints of modern life call for a new approach to entertaining. "Can I make that ahead?" is the question we are most often asked at the cookery classes we teach.

A canapé party is a practical way for both experienced and beginner cooks to entertain at home. A large number of guests can be accommodated without matching dinner service, tables or even chairs. Piles of dirty pans, plates and cutlery cluttering up the sink are not a burden, because canapés are easily hand held and simply eaten with only a small paper serviette. There's no need to worry about spending all day or all night in the kitchen. Canapés are flexible foods that can be prepared well ahead of time.

We set out to create a cook book that puts the pleasure back into entertaining. We have included practical tips, techniques and timing that we hope will inspire you to invite your friends and family to celebrate.

We don't want to turn home cooks into professional caterers. We want to help home cooks be confident cooks, because confident cooks make happy hosts, and happy hosts give great parties.

So, relax. Because everybody loves a party, and home-cooked food always makes an occasion special.

Eric   Arora

Notes From the Cooks

BEFORE YOU COOK read through the recipe carefully. Make sure you have all the equipment and ingredients required.

On Measuring

Accurate measurements are essential if you want the same good results each time you make a recipe. We have given measurements in metric and imperial in all the recipes. Always stick to one set of measurements; never use a mixture of both in the same recipe.

A kitchen scale is the most accurate way to measure dry ingredients. We recommend using scales for all except the smallest amounts.

We recommend using cooks' measuring spoons when following a recipe. All spoon measurements in the book are level unless otherwise stated. To measure dry ingredients with a spoon; scoop the ingredient lightly from the storage container, then level the surface with the edge of a straight-bladed knife.

We use standard level spoon measurements
1 tbsp – 15ml (½ floz)
1 tsp – 5ml (⅙ floz)

For maximum accuracy when using graduated measuring cups for dry ingredients, spoon the ingredient loosely into the required cup, mounding it up slightly, then level the surface with the edge of a straight-bladed knife. Do not use the cup as a scoop, pack the ingredient into the cup or tap the cup on the work surface. This will give you an inaccurate result.

To measure liquids, choose a transparent glass or plastic measuring jug. Always place the jug on a flat surface and check for accuracy at eye level when pouring in a liquid to measure.

A final and important rule of measuring – never measure ingredients over the mixing bowl!

On Oven Temperatures

Always preheat your oven for 10–20 minutes before you will need to use it. This allows it to reach the required temperature. Bear in mind that the higher the temperature required, the longer it will take to preheat the oven.

Ovens vary from kitchen to kitchen. Most have hot spots, so be prepared to rotate dishes from top to bottom or from front to back during the cooking time. A good oven thermometer is an important piece of kitchen equipment.

If using a fan assisted oven, follow the manufacturer's instructions for adjusting cooking timings and oven temperatures.

On Quantities

However accurate we measure, cookery remains to some extent an unpredictable science. Ingredients vary, so use the yields we give for each recipe as general guidelines. Canapés are bite-size morsels that should be eaten in one mouthful, so be prepared to modify the number of items the recipe yields to suit this criteria. We have done our best to ensure that none of the recipes yield less than the quantity stated, but in some cases a recipe might make a few extra, which will of course allow for both breakage – and tasting!

On Tasting

Always taste food as you cook and before you serve. Don't be afraid to add or change flavours to suit your palate – what's fun about cooking is experimenting, improvising, creating. Ingredients differ from day to day, season to season, kitchen to kitchen; our tomato may be a little riper than your tomato, and so on. Be prepared to the adjust sweetness, sharpness, spiciness, and, most important of all, salt to your own taste.

READY-MADE FOR GETTING AHEAD

Make use of ready-made bases, cases and sauces to save time and relieve pre-party pressure.
Look for these at gourmet stores and in larger supermarkets.

1 Mayonnaise
2 Bouchée cases
3 Chocolate cups
4 Croustades
5 Filo pastry
6 Hollandaise
7 Puff pastry
8 Pesto
9 Pastry cases
10 Flour tortillas

FINE FOODS FOR SPECIAL OCCASIONS

Celebrations call for a little luxury. Indulge family and friends with ingredients of the highest quality and throw in some of these gourmet treats.

1. Parmesan cheese
2. Stilton cheese
3. Roquefort cheese
4. Quail eggs
5. Lobster
6. Black lumpfish roe
7. Red lumpfish roe
8. Salmon roe
9. Caviar
10. Medium prawns
11. Tiger prawns
12. Queen scallops
13. Sea scallops
14. Crab claw
15. Smoked salmon
16. Proscuitto
17. Oyster

BOLD FLAVOURS FOR BITE-SIZED MORSELS

Canapés are tiny mouthfuls of food designed to stimulate the appetite and whet the thirst. Raid the global larder for sweet, sharp, spicy, salty and sour flavours and remember to season with a generous hand.

1. Lemon, lime and orange zest
2. Thai sweet chilli sauce
3. Chinese hot chilli sauce
4. Tabasco
5. Balsamic vinegar
6. Worcestershire sauce
7. Curry powder
8. Paprika
9. Crushed chilli flakes
10. Cayenne
11. Sesame seeds
12. Pickled ginger
13. Horseradish sauce
14. Olives
15. Anchovy fillets
16. Chipotles in adobo
17. Grainy mustard
18. Mustard powder
19. Creamy Dijon mustard
20. Chilli peppers
21. Fresh herbs
22. Baby capers
23. Capers

KITCHEN TOOLS

A good, sharp knife, a selection of pastry cutters, a melon baller and a piping bag with tubes will create myriad professional-looking canapé items.

1. 2.5cm (1in) fluted pastry cutter
2. 5cm (2in) fluted pastry cutter
3. 4.5cm (1¾in) fluted pastry cutter
4. 6.5cm (2¾in) plain pastry cutter
5. 5cm (2in) plain pastry cutter
6. 3.5cm (1½in) plain pastry cutter
7. 6cm (2½in) star-shaped pastry cutter
8. 6cm (2½in) heart-shaped cutter
9. 3.5cm (1⅜in) heart-shaped pastry cutter
10. Vegetable peeler
11. Oyster knife
12. Melon baller
13. Zester
14. Stoner
15. Serrated knife
16. Chef's knife
17. Kitchen scissors
18. Large star piping nozzle
19. Large plain piping nozzle

1. Plain tartlet tin
2. Baking sheet
3. Mini muffin tins
4. Fluted tartlet tins
5. Oven tray

BAKEWARE

Flat baking sheets, rimmed oven trays and mini muffin tins are the most essential bakeware in the canapé kitchen. Continental tartlet tins are a bonus, since they make the daintiest pastry cases, but mini muffin tins work well too.

THE RECIPES

READ THROUGH THE RECIPE FIRST.

USE FRESH SEASONAL INGREDIENTS.

HAVE FUN – YOU'RE COOKING FOR A PARTY.

NIBBLES, DIPS AND DIPPERS

SPICED PARTY NUTS

Makes 500ml (¾ pint)
250g (8oz) skinned almonds
1 tbsp egg white, about ½ an egg white
2 tsp dark brown sugar
2 tsp salt
½ tsp cayenne pepper
1 tbsp finely chopped rosemary

Preheat oven to 150°C (300°F) Gas 2.
Spread nuts in a single layer on an
oven tray. Roast, shaking the tray
occasionally, until lightly golden, 15
minutes. Remove from oven and cool
slightly. Whisk egg white until frothy
and add nuts, sugar, salt, cayenne and
rosemary. Toss ingredients together to
coat each nut well. Return nuts to the
oven. Roast until fragrant and golden,
20 minutes. Cool. Serve at room
temperature.

THINK AHEAD
Make up to 3 days in advance. Cool and store in an
airtight container at room temperature. Alternatively,
freeze up to 1 month in advance (see page 149).
Defrost overnight in refrigerator. Crisp in a
preheated 180°C (350°F) Gas 4 oven, 3 minutes.

COOKS' NOTE
To make curried almonds omit sugar, cayenne and
rosemary and replace with 1tbsp curry powder.

CRUNCHY SWEET AND SPICY PECANS

MAKES 500ml (¾ pint)
250g (8oz) pecans
1 tbsp sunflower oil
4 tbsp sugar
1 tsp salt
1½ tsp chilli powder

Preheat oven to 150°C (300°F) Gas 2.
Spread pecans on an oven tray. Roast,
shaking the tray occasionally, until nutty
and toasted, 30 minutes. Heat the oil in
a frying pan over a medium heat. Add
nuts and stir to coat. Sprinkle with
sugar and salt. Cook, stirring constantly,
until the sugar melts and starts to brown
slightly, 5 minutes. Remove from heat
but continue stirring until cooled
slightly. Sprinkle over chilli powder and
toss to coat each nut well. Serve at room
temperature.

THINK AHEAD
Make up to 3 days in advance. Cool and store in an
airtight container at room temperature. Alternatively,
freeze up to 1 month in advance (see page 149).
Defrost overnight in refrigerator. Crisp in a
preheated 180°C (350°F) Gas 4 oven, 3 minutes.

COOKS' NOTE
Use the variety of chilli powders now available at
gourmet food shops to achieve slightly different
flavours. Ancho chilli powder will add a hint of
smoky flavour to this piquant mixture.

MEDITERRANEAN MARINATED OLIVES

MAKES 500ml (¾ pint)
250g (8oz) black or green olives
or a mixture
1 tsp fennel seeds
½ tsp cumin seeds
grated zest of ½ orange
grated zest of ½ lemon
2 garlic cloves, finely chopped
2 tsp crushed chilli flakes
1 tsp dried oregano
1 tbsp lemon juice
1 tbsp red wine vinegar
2 tbsp olive oil
1 tbsp finely chopped parsley

If desired, pit olives. Toast fennel and
cumin seeds in a dry pan over a low
heat until aromatic, 2 minutes.
Combine seeds, olives, zests, garlic,
chilli, oregano, lemon, vinegar and oil
and toss to coat each olive well. Place in
an airtight container. Leave to marinate
at room temperature for 8 hours. Shake
the container occasionally to remix the
ingredients, while marinating. Stir in
the parsley. Serve at room temperature.

THINK AHEAD
Make up to 1 week in advance, omitting the parsley.
Store in an airtight container and refrigerate. Add
parsley up to 3 hours before serving.

COOKS' NOTE
Warming the olives will intensify the flavours.
Gently heat the marinated olives over a low heat
until warmed through, 5 minutes. Serve warm.

SAVOURY SABLES

MAKES 40

250g (8oz) plain flour
175g (6oz) cold butter, diced
250g (8oz) gruyère cheese
¼ tsp cayenne pepper

¼ tsp mustard powder
1 egg yolk beaten with
1 tbsp water

ESSENTIAL EQUIPMENT
6cm (2½in) star-shaped pastry cutter, 6cm (2½in) heart-shaped pastry cutter, baking parchment

Place flour, butter, cheese, cayenne and mustard powder in a food processor; pulse until the mixture forms a pastry. Add a little cold water (1 tsp at a time) as necessary to bring the pastry together.
Roll out pastry on a floured surface to a 0.5cm (¼in) thickness.
Stamp out into decorative shapes with pastry cutters. Place 2cm (¾in) apart on 2 baking parchment lined baking sheets.
Refrigerate cut pastry shapes until firm, 30 minutes.
Preheat oven to 180°C (350°F) Gas 4.
Brush with beaten egg. Bake until golden brown, 10 minutes.
Cool on a wire rack. Serve warm or at room temperature, with or without dips.

THINK AHEAD
Make sablés up to 2 weeks in advance. Store in an airtight container at room temperature. Alternatively, make and freeze up to 1 month in advance (see page 149). Defrost and crisp for 3 minutes in preheated 200°C (400°F) Gas 6 oven.

FLAVOURED SABLE VARIATIONS

SPICY SABLES
Place 2 tsp paprika with the other ingredients in the food processor.

SEEDED SABLES
Omit mustard powder. Place 2 tsp caraway seeds with the other ingredients in the food processor.

HERBED SABLES
Omit mustard powder. Place 2 tsp finely chopped rosemary with the other ingredients in the food processor.

ROQUEFORT SABLES
Omit mustard powder and cayenne. Use a combination of 125g (4oz) crumbled roquefort cheese and 125g (4oz) grated gruyère instead of 250g (8oz) grated gruyère.

SWISS CHEESE ALLUMETTES

MAKES 30

125g (4oz) plain flour
90g (3oz) cold butter, diced
1 egg yolk
125g (4oz) gruyère cheese, grated
salt, black pepper, cayenne pepper
1 egg beaten with 1 tbsp water
1 tbsp grated parmesan cheese

ESSENTIAL EQUIPMENT
baking parchment

Place flour, butter, egg yolk and cheese with a pinch each of salt, pepper and cayenne in a food processor; pulse until the mixture forms a firm pastry. Turn out and knead lightly by hand until smooth.
Roll out pastry on a floured surface to a 0.5cm (¼in) thickness. Cut into strips about 1cm (½in) wide and 7cm (3in) long. Place 2cm (¾in) apart on baking sheets lined with baking parchment. Refrigerate until firm, 30 minutes.
Preheat oven to 180°C (350°F) Gas 4.
Brush with beaten egg. Sprinkle with parmesan. Bake until golden brown, 15 minutes. Cool on a wire rack.
Serve warm or at room temperature, with or without dips.

THINK AHEAD
Make allumettes up to 2 weeks in advance. Store in an airtight container at room temperature. Alternatively, make and freeze up to 1 month in advance (see page 149). Defrost and crisp for 3 minutes in preheated 200°C (400°F) Gas 6 oven.

TRIPLE CHOCOLATE BISCOTTINI WITH HAZELNUTS

MAKES 50

200g (7oz) plain flour
60g (2oz) cocoa powder
¾ tsp baking powder
¼ tsp salt
150g (5oz) caster sugar

ESSENTIAL EQUIPMENT
paper piping bag (see page 146)

60g (2oz) dark chocolate, chopped
3 eggs, beaten
1 tsp vanilla extract
100g (3½oz) hazelnuts, skinned
(see page 163)
100g (3½oz) white chocolate to garnish

Preheat oven 180°C (350°F) Gas 4.
Sift flour, cocoa, baking powder and salt into a bowl. Add sugar, chocolate, eggs and vanilla and mix with a fork to form a rough dough. Alternatively, place flour, cocoa, baking powder, salt, sugar, chocolate, eggs and vanilla in a food processor; pulse to form a rough dough.
Knead the hazelnuts into the dough with hands. Divide the dough into 4 equal-sized pieces. Shape each piece into logs, 2.5cm (1in) thick and 30cm (12in) long. Place logs on floured baking sheets. Bake until firm to the touch, 25 minutes. Remove and leave until cool enough to handle. With a serrated knife, cut each biscotti log on the diagonal into 1cm (½in) thick slices. Place the slices in a single layer on baking sheets. Bake until crisp and dry, 15 minutes. Cool on a wire rack. Melt the white chocolate (see page 145). Fill piping bag with chocolate. Drizzle over the biscottini.

THINK AHEAD
Make up to 2 weeks in advance. Store in an airtight container at room temperature. Alternatively, freeze the unbaked biscotti logs up to 1 month in advance (see page 149). Defrost overnight in the refrigerator before baking.

COOKS' NOTE
For an alternative finish, try dipping one end of each biscottini into the melted white chocolate.

PARMESAN AND PINE NUT BISCOTTINI WITH GREEN OLIVES

MAKES 50

100g (3½oz) pine nuts
250g (8oz) plain flour
1 tsp baking powder
1 tsp salt
¼ tsp black pepper
1 tbsp fennel seeds
2 tbsp grated parmesan cheese
100g (3½oz) pitted green olives,
finely chopped
3 eggs, beaten

Preheat oven to 180°C (350°F) Gas 4.
Spread pine nuts in a single layer on an oven tray. Toast in oven until nutty and golden, 7 minutes. Cool.
Sift flour, baking powder and salt into a bowl. Add pepper, fennel seeds, parmesan, olives and eggs and mix with a fork to form a rough dough. Alternatively, place flour, baking powder, salt, pepper, fennel seeds, parmesan, olives and eggs in a food processor; pulse to a rough dough.
Knead the pine nuts into the dough with hands. Divide dough into 4 equal-sized pieces. Shape each piece into a log, 2.5cm (1in) thick and 30cm (12in) long. Place each log on a floured baking sheet.
Bake until firm to the touch, 25 minutes. Remove and leave until cool enough to handle. With a serrated knife, cut each biscotti log on the diagonal into 1cm (½in) thick slices. Place the slices in a single layer on the baking sheets. Bake until crisp and dry, 15 minutes. Cool completely on a wire rack.

THINK AHEAD
Make up to 2 weeks in advance. Store in an airtight container at room temperature. Alternatively, freeze the unbaked biscotti logs up to 1 month in advance (see page 149). Defrost overnight in the refrigerator before baking.

CURRY PUFFS

MAKES 35

1 recipe unbaked choux pastry
(see page 138)
1 tsp cumin seeds
2 tsp curry powder
1 tsp turmeric
¼ tsp cayenne pepper
½ onion, grated

Preheat oven to 180°C (350°F) Gas 4.
Toast cumin seeds in a dry pan over a
low heat until fragrant, 3 minutes.
Stir toasted spices and onion into pastry.
Drop teaspoonfuls on to an oiled baking
sheet. Bake until golden, 30 minutes.
Serve warm.

THINK AHEAD
Bake up to 3 days in advance. Store in an airtight
container at room temperature. Crisp in preheated
200°C (400°F) Gas 6 oven, 3 minutes.
Alternatively, bake and freeze up to 1 month in
advance (see page 149). Defrost. Crisp as directed.

CHORIZO PUFFS

MAKES 35

125g (4oz) chorizo sausage, skinned and
finely chopped
1 recipe unbaked choux pastry
(see page 138)

Preheat oven to 180°C (350°F) Gas 4.
Stir chorizo into pastry. Drop
teaspoonfuls on to an oiled baking sheet.
Bake until golden, 30 minutes.
Serve warm.

THINK AHEAD
Bake up to 3 days in advance. Store in an airtight
container at room temperature. Crisp in preheated
200°C (400°F) Gas 6 oven, 3 minutes.
Alternatively, bake and freeze up to 1 month in
advance (see page 149). Defrost. Crisp as directed.

MINI GOUGERES

MAKES 30

100g (3½oz) grated gruyère cheese
1 recipe unbaked choux pastry
(see page 138)

ESSENTIAL EQUIPMENT
piping bag with large, plain tube

Preheat oven to 180°C (350°F) Gas 4.
Stir half of the cheese into the pastry.
Fill piping bag with pastry (see page
146) and pipe out rings, each one about
5cm (2in) in diameter, on to an oiled
baking sheet. Sprinkle with remaining
cheese. Bake until golden, 30 minutes.
Serve warm.

THINK AHEAD
Bake up to 3 days in advance. Store in an airtight
container at room temperature. Crisp in preheated
200°C (400°F) Gas 6 oven, 3 minutes.
Alternatively, bake and freeze up to 1 month in
advance (see page 149). Defrost. Crisp as directed.

PARMESAN AND ANCHOVY PALMIERS

MAKES 20
250g (8oz) puff pastry
50g (1¾oz) drained anchovy fillets,
finely chopped
¼ tsp black pepper
2 tbsp grated parmesan cheese
1 egg yolk beaten with 1 tbsp water

Preheat oven to 200°C (400°F) Gas 6.
Roll pastry to 15cm x 35cm (6in x 14in)
rectangle. Trim uneven edges with a
sharp knife. Spread anchovies evenly
over pastry. Sprinkle with pepper and
parmesan. Roll up ends tightly to meet
in the middle of pastry (see below).
Refrigerate until firm, 20 minutes.
Brush with beaten egg on all sides. Cut
across into 1cm (½in) thick slices. Place
slices on an oiled baking sheet. Bake
until crisp and golden, 10 minutes. Cool
on wire rack. Serve warm or at room
temperature.

THINK AHEAD
Same as recipes opposite.

Rolling up pastry
for palmiers.

SUN-DRIED TOMATO PESTO PALMIERS

MAKES 20
6 sun-dried tomatoes in oil,
drained (reserve oil) and finely chopped
1 garlic clove, crushed
1 tbsp reserved oil from sun-dried
tomatoes
3 tbsp grated parmesan cheese
250g (8oz) puff pastry
1 egg yolk beaten with 1 tbsp water

Preheat oven to 200°C (400°F) Gas 6.
For pesto, mix tomatoes, garlic, reserved
oil and 2 tbsp parmesan until well
combined. Roll pastry to 15cm x 35cm
(6in x 14in) rectangle. Trim uneven
edges with sharp knife. Spread pesto
evenly over pastry. Roll up ends tightly
to meet in the middle of pastry (see
below, left). Refrigerate until firm,
20 minutes. Brush with beaten egg on
all sides. Cut across into 1cm (½in) thick
slices. Place slices on an oiled baking
sheet. Bake until crisp and golden,
10 minutes. Sprinkle over remaining
parmesan when hot from oven. Cool
on wire rack. Serve warm or at room
temperature.

THINK AHEAD
Bake up to 3 days in advance. Crisp in preheated
200°C (400°F) Gas 6, 3 minutes. Store in an airtight
container at room temperature. Alternatively, freeze
unbaked (see page 149). Bake from frozen in
preheated 200°C (400°F) Gas 6 for 15 minutes.

HONEY MUSTARD AND PROSCIUTTO PALMIERS

MAKES 20
250g (8oz) puff pastry
2 tsp creamy Dijon mustard
4 tsp runny honey
75g (2½oz) sliced prosciutto
3 tbsp grated parmesan cheese
1 egg yolk beaten with 1 tbsp water

Preheat oven to 200°C (400°F) Gas 6.
Roll pastry to 15cm x 35cm (6in x 14in)
rectangle. Trim uneven edges with sharp
knife. Combine mustard and honey.
Spread evenly over pastry. Cover with
sliced prosciutto. Sprinkle with 2 tbsp
parmesan. Roll up ends tightly to meet
in the middle of pastry (see below, far
left). Refrigerate until firm, 20 minutes.
Brush with beaten egg on all sides. Cut
across into 1cm (½in) slices. Place slices
on an oiled baking sheet. Bake until
crisp and golden, 10 minutes. Sprinkle
over remaining parmesan when hot from
oven. Cool on wire rack. Serve warm
or at room temperature.

THINK AHEAD
Bake up to 3 days in advance. Crisp in preheated
200°C (400°F) Gas 6, 3 minutes. Store in an airtight
container at room temperature. Alternatively, freeze
unbaked (see page 149). Bake from frozen in
preheated 200°C (400°F) Gas 6 for 15 minutes.

TWISTED PARSLEY BREADSTICKS

MAKES 35

1 recipe unbaked bread dough (see page 140)
100g (3½oz) red leicester or other hard orange cheese
15g (½oz) flat-leaf parsley, roughly chopped
¼ tsp cayenne pepper

Preheat oven to 200°C (400°F) Gas 6. Roll out dough to 15cm x 50cm (6in x 20in) rectangle. Sprinkle over cheese, parsley and cayenne. Fold dough in half widthwise. Roll dough lightly to press in the filling and compress the two layers together. With a sharp knife, cut dough across into 0.5cm (¼in) wide strips. Hold ends of each strip between your fingers and twist ends in opposite directions. Lay twisted strips on to oiled baking sheets (see below). Bake until crisp and golden, 15 minutes. Cool on wire rack. Serve warm or at room temperature.

THINK AHEAD
Bake up to 3 days in advance. Store in an airtight container at room temperature. Crisp in preheated 200°C (400°F) Gas 6 oven, 3 minutes.

PARMESAN CHEESE STRAWS

MAKES 40

250g (8oz) puff pastry
2 tsp paprika
3 tbsp grated parmesan cheese
1 egg yolk beaten with 1 tbsp water

Preheat oven to 200°C (400°F) Gas 6. Roll out pastry to 15cm x 50cm (6in x 20in) triangle. Sprinkle over paprika and 2 tbsp of the parmesan. Spread cheese with your hands to evenly cover pastry. Fold pastry in half widthways. Brush folded pastry with beaten egg. Sprinkle over remaining parmesan. Press lightly into the pastry with hands to secure the cheese.

With a sharp knife, cut pastry across into 0.5cm (¼in) wide strips. Hold ends of each strip between your fingers and twist ends in opposite directions (see below, left). Lay twisted strips on to oiled baking sheets. Bake until crisp and golden, 7 minutes. Cool on wire racks. Serve warm or at room temperature.

THINK AHEAD
Bake up to 3 days in advance. Store in airtight container at room temperature. Crisp in preheated 200°C (400°F) Gas 6 oven, 3 minutes.

VEGETABLE DIPPERS

Prepare your chosen vegetables as directed. Arrange vegetables in an airtight container covered with damp paper towels. Cover with the lid and refrigerate. Serve chilled, with dips.

BABY CARROTS Choose firm, crisp baby carrots and use as quickly as possible as they spoil more quickly than regular carrots. Do not peel. Trim root end but leave a short green stem to act as a handle for dipping.

BABY POTATOES Choose even-sized, small new potatoes with a crisp, waxy texture and papery, thin skins. Simmer, unpeeled, in salted water until tender when pierced with the tip of a small sharp knife. Use gold and red skinned potatoes for added colour contrast.

CARROTS Avoid large carrots as they may have a tough, woody core. Organically grown carrots have the sweetest flavour. Cut into sticks about 8cm (3in) long and 0.5cm (¼in) thick.

CELERY Use only the pale, tender inner stalks. The outer stalks tend to be stringy and should be peeled. Cut into sticks about 8cm (3in) long and 0.5cm (¼in) thick.

CHICORY Trim the bitter stem end and use only the crisp, smaller inner leaves. Chicory is grown in red as well as white varieties.

CHERRY TOMATOES Try and find yellow as well as red for colour contrast. The plum and pear shaped cherry tomato varieties are now widely available. Their elongated shape makes them easier to use for dipping.

CUCUMBERS Scrape out the seeds and discard. Cut into sticks about 8cm (3in) long and 0.5cm (¼in) thick. Leave unpeeled for added colour contrast between the dark green peel and pearly pale green interior.

RADISHES Trim the root end but leave a little green stem on to act as a handle for dipping. Elongated French-style varieties with red tops and white tips are best for dipping.

THINK AHEAD
Prepare vegetables up to 1 day in advance.

COOKS' NOTE
A generous quantity of just one or two vegetables makes an impressive display. Choose vegetables that are at their freshest, seasonal best, rather than aiming for a lavish selection.

FORMING TWISTED STRIPS
Twist ends in opposite directions

OVEN-DRIED ROOT AND FRUIT CHIPS

MAKES 150g (5oz)

1 small sweet potato, unpeeled
1 small beetroot, unpeeled
1 small parsnip, unpeeled
1 apple, unpeeled
1 pear, unpeeled
2 tsp salt

ESSENTIAL EQUIPMENT
either a food processor with a slicing attachment, a mandoline or a Japanese vegetable slicer

Preheat oven to 180°C (350°F) Gas 4. Use either the slicing attachment on a food processor, mandoline or Japanese vegetable slicer to slice the unpeeled sweet potato, beetroot, parsnip, apple and pear 2mm (⅛in thick). Place slices in a single layer on oiled baking sheets. Put into the oven. Reduce oven temperature to 120°C (250°F) Gas ½. Bake for 1½ hours, turning the slices over every 20 minutes, until dried. Cool in single layers on wire racks. Sprinkle with salt. Serve at room temperature, with or without dips.

THINK AHEAD
Make up to 1 day in advance. Store in an airtight container at room temperature.

CRISPY POTATO SKINS

MAKES 40

5 medium potatoes, pricked
2 tbsp olive oil
1 tbsp finely chopped fresh rosemary
or 2 tsp crumbled dried rosemary
1½ tsp salt
1 tsp black pepper

Preheat oven to 180°C (350°F) Gas 4. Bake potatoes until tender, 1 hour. Cool. Cut each potato into 6 wedges. Scoop out the cooked potato, leaving the skins intact and a shell of potato and skin, about 0.5cm (¼in) thick. If desired, reserve cooked potato for another use. Brush potato skins with oil on both sides. Place in a single layer scooped side up on to a wire rack set on top of an oven tray. Sprinkle evenly with rosemary, salt and pepper. Bake for 15 minutes, then remove from oven and turn skins over. Return skins to the oven and continue baking until crisp and golden brown, 15 minutes. Serve at room temperature, with or without dips.

THINK AHEAD
Make up to 1 day in advance. Store in an airtight container at room temperature.

COOK'S NOTE
Make this recipe the day before your party and use the reserved cooked potato to make a delicious potato mash for supper the night before.

HERBED PITA CRISPS

MAKES 40

2 garlic cloves, crushed
6 tbsp olive oil
4 pita breads, white, brown or a mixture
2 tbsp fresh thyme leaves
or 2 tsp dried thyme
1½ tsp salt
1 tsp black pepper

ESSENTIAL EQUIPMENT
kitchen scissors or a serrated knife

Preheat oven to 180°C (350°F) Gas 4. Stir garlic into oil. Cut each pita into 5 strips with scissors or a serrated knife. Snip end of each strip and separate to make 2 single layer strips. Place pita strips split side up in a single layer on baking sheets. Brush with garlic olive oil. Sprinkle evenly with thyme, salt and pepper. Bake until crisp and golden brown, 15 minutes. Cool. Serve at room temperature with or without dips.

THINK AHEAD
Make up to 2 days in advance. Store in an airtight container at room temperature.

COOKS' NOTE
To make spiced pita crisps, sprinkle pita with 2 tsp each cumin and sesame seeds instead of thyme leaves.

CHICKEN DRUMMETTES

20 chicken wings

ESSENTIAL EQUIPMENT
kitchen scissors or sharp boning knife

Cut the first joint of each chicken wing and discard wing tips. Holding small end of second joint, cut, scrape and push meat down to thick end (see right). Pull skin and meat over end of bone with fingers to resemble baby drumsticks. Cut off knuckle end with scissors or knife. Repeat with remaining chicken wings.

THINK AHEAD
Make drummettes up to 2 days in advance. Cover and refrigerate.

COOKS' NOTE
The tips and first joint of chicken wings are basically just skin and bone. When making drummettes, reserve these parts for later use. They are ideal for making chicken stock.

HONEY MUSTARD CHICKEN DRUMMETTES

MAKES 20
8 garlic cloves, crushed
2 tbsp runny honey
2 tbsp creamy Dijon mustard
2 tbsp light soy sauce
2 tbsp lemon juice
4 tbsp olive oil
2 tsp salt
1 tsp black pepper
1 recipe chicken drummettes (see above)

Combine garlic, honey, mustard, soy sauce, lemon, oil, salt and pepper in a non-metallic bowl. Add chicken and toss to coat each piece well. Cover and refrigerate for at least 1 hour.
Preheat oven to 180°C (350°F) Gas 4. Place chicken on a wire rack set over an oven tray. Bake until chicken is well browned and cooked through, 35 minutes.
Serve warm or at room temperature, with or without dips.

THINK AHEAD
Marinate chicken up to 1 day in advance. Cover and refrigerate.

GINGER HOISIN CHICKEN DRUMMETTES

MAKES 20
10cm (4in) piece fresh ginger, grated
2 garlic cloves, crushed
6 tbsp hoisin sauce
1 tbsp Chinese hot chilli sauce
1 tbsp light soy sauce
1 tbsp granulated sugar
1 tbsp water
1 recipe chicken drummettes (see above)

Combine ginger, garlic, sauces, sugar and water in a non-metallic bowl. Add chicken and toss to coat each piece well. Cover and refrigerate for at least 1 hour.
Preheat oven to 180°C (350°F) Gas 4. Place chicken on a wire rack set over an oven tray. Bake until chicken is well browned and cooked through, 35 minutes.
Serve warm or at room temperature, with or without dips.

THINK AHEAD
Marinate chicken up to 1 day in advance. Cover and refrigerate.

HONEY SESAME GLAZED COCKTAIL SAUSAGES

MAKES ABOUT 30
500g (1lb) cocktail sausages, separated
1 tbsp sesame seeds
½ tbsp runny honey

Preheat oven to 180°C (350°F) Gas 4. Arrange the sausages in a single layer on an oiled oven tray. Bake for 20 minutes, then turn sausages over on the tray. Roast until golden and cooked through, 15 minutes. Sprinkle with sesame seeds and drizzle with honey. Toss to coat each sausage well. Serve hot or warm, with or without dips.

THINK AHEAD
Cook sausages up to 12 hours in advance. Cool and cover with tin foil. Reheat in 200°C (400°F) Gas 6 oven, 10 minutes. Alternatively, cook sausages up to 1 hour in advance. Cover with foil and keep warm. Toss with seeds and honey just before serving.

COOKS' NOTE
Any good butcher that makes chipolata sausages will make cocktail sausages to order.

COCKTAIL SAUSAGE VARIATIONS

HONEY ROSEMARY GLAZED COCKTAIL SAUSAGES
Replace sesame seeds with 2 tsp finely chopped rosemary.

SWEET AND SPICY GLAZED COCKTAIL SAUSAGES
Replace honey and sesame seeds with 1½ tbsp mango chutney.

CURRY SPICED YOGHURT, CORIANDER AND MANGO CHUTNEY DIP

MAKES ABOUT 500ml (¾ pint)

6 tbsp mango chutney
15g (½ oz) coriander, chopped
4 spring onions, chopped
juice of 2 limes
175g (6oz) cream cheese
250g (8oz) Greek-style yoghurt
½ tsp curry powder
¼ tsp turmeric
salt, Tabasco

Place chutney, coriander, spring onions, lime, cream cheese, yoghurt and spices in a food processor or blender; pulse until well blended. Add salt and Tabasco to taste. Cover and refrigerate for 30 minutes to allow the flavours to blend. Serve chilled with dippers.

THINK AHEAD
Make dip up to 1 day in advance. Cover and refrigerate.

COOKS' NOTE
Make this creamy yoghurt dip Thai-style: omit the curry powder and replace the mango chutney with the same amount of Thai sweet chilli sauce.

SALSA ROMESCO DIP

MAKES ABOUT 500ml (¾ pint)

1 red pepper, quartered and seeded
1 tbsp olive oil
75g (2½oz) skinned almonds
5cm (2in) thick slice of day-old bread, cubed
2 garlic cloves, chopped
¼ tsp cayenne pepper
½ tsp paprika
15g (½oz) parsley, chopped
2 tomatoes, chopped
2 tbsp sherry vinegar
salt, black pepper

Grill and peel pepper quarters (see page 147). Heat oil in pan over a medium heat. Stir-fry almonds and bread cubes until golden, 5 minutes. Drain on kitchen paper. Place peeled pepper quarters, almonds, bread, garlic, spices, parsley, tomatoes and vinegar in a food processor or blender; pulse until well blended but still retaining some texture. If necessary, adjust the consistency by gradually adding water 1 tbsp at a time. Add salt and pepper to taste. Cover and refrigerate for 30 minutes to allow the flavours to blend. Serve chilled with dippers.

THINK AHEAD
Make dip up to 3 days in advance. Cover and refrigerate.

COOKS' NOTES
You don't have to restrict yourself to using almonds in this piquant Catalan sauce. You can use hazelnuts, pine nuts, or a combination of either with the almonds, with equal authenticity.

ROAST RED PEPPER, FETA AND MINT DIP

MAKES ABOUT 500ml (¾ pint)

3 red peppers, quartered and seeded
200g (7oz) feta cheese
200g (7oz) cream cheese
1 garlic clove, chopped
3 tbsp fresh mint, finely chopped
2 tbsp olive oil
1 tbsp lemon juice
salt, black pepper

Grill and peel pepper quarters (see page 147). Place peeled pepper quarters, feta and cream cheese, garlic, mint, oil and lemon juice in a food processor or blender; pulse until well blended but still retaining some texture. If necessary, adjust consistency by gradually adding water 1 tbsp at a time. Add salt and pepper to taste. Cover and refrigerate for 30 minutes to allow the flavours to blend. Serve chilled with dippers.

THINK AHEAD
Make dip up to 3 days in advance. Cover and refrigerate.

AVOCADO LIME CREAM DIP

MAKES ABOUT 500ml (¾ pint)

2 medium avocados
4 spring onions, chopped
2 green chillies, seeded and finely chopped
15g (½oz) coriander
juice of 2 limes
1 tbsp olive oil
150ml (5floz) sour cream
salt

Place avocado, spring onions, chillies, coriander, lime, olive oil and sour cream in a food processor or blender; pulse until smooth. Add salt to taste. Cover and refrigerate for 15 minutes to allow the flavours to blend. Serve chilled with dippers.

THINK AHEAD
Make dip up to 8 hours ahead. Cover and refrigerate.

COOKS' NOTE
To prevent the avocado cream dip from discolouring, make sure you press a piece of cling film directly on to the surface of the dip. It's the oxygen in the air that turns avocado brown, so the less air that comes into contact with the dip, the better.

HERBED YOGHURT DIP

MAKES ABOUT 500ml (¾ pint)
15g (½oz) parsley, chopped
15g (½oz) basil, chopped
15g (½oz) chives, chopped
grated zest of ½ lemon
juice of 1 lemon
175g (6oz) cream cheese
250g (8oz) Greek-style yoghurt
3 tbsp olive oil
salt, black pepper

Place herbs, lemon, cream cheese, yoghurt and oil in a food processor or blender; pulse until well blended. Add salt and pepper to taste. Cover and refrigerate for 30 minutes to allow the flavours to blend. Serve chilled.

THINK AHEAD
Make dip up to 1 day in advance. Cover and refrigerate.

COOKS' NOTE
Use your favourite bouquet of green herbs to flavour this fragrant dip. Choose from rocket, tarragon, marjoram, chervil, watercress or lovage instead of one or all of our favourite combination of parsley, basil and chives.
For a lighter dip, use ricotta cheese in place of some or all of the cream cheese.

CREAMY BLUE CHEESE AND SPRING ONION DIP

MAKES ABOUT 500ml (¾ pint)
6 spring onions, chopped
200g (7oz) blue cheese (see cooks' note)
300ml (10floz) sour cream
1 tsp Worcestershire sauce
salt, black pepper

Place spring onions, cheese, sour cream and Worcestershire sauce in a food processor or blender; pulse until well blended but still retaining some texture. If necessary, adjust consistency by gradually adding water 1 tbsp at a time. Add salt and pepper to taste. Cover and refrigerate for 30 minutes to allow the flavours to blend. Serve chilled.

THINK AHEAD
Make dip up to 1 day in advance. Cover and refrigerate. Let stand at room temperature for 5 minutes to soften slightly before serving.

COOKS' NOTE
Your choice of blue cheese will determine the richness and piquancy of this delicious dip. Use roquefort, gorgonzola or stilton to intensify its zesty, pungent flavour. Try dolcelatte or danish blue to make a dip with a milder, mellower taste.

SUN-DRIED TOMATO AND CANNELLINI BEAN DIP

MAKES ABOUT 500ml (¾ pint)
400g (14oz) tinned cannellini beans, drained
8 sun-dried tomatoes in oil, drained
1 garlic clove, chopped
1 tbsp rosemary, chopped
4 tbsp olive oil
2 tbsp red wine vinegar
125ml (4floz) water
salt, black pepper

Place beans, sun-dried tomatoes, garlic, rosemary, oil, vinegar and water in a food processor or blender; pulse to a smooth purée. If necessary, adjust the consistency by gradually adding more water, 1 tbsp at a time. Add salt and pepper to taste. Cover and refrigerate for 30 minutes to allow the flavours to blend. Serve chilled.

THINK AHEAD
Make dip up to 3 days in advance. Cover and refrigerate.

COOKS' NOTE
Cannellini are slender, ivory white Italian beans. Their creamy texture and their ability to absorb strong, aromatic flavours makes them ideal for dips. If you cannot find a source for cannellini beans, any tinned white bean will make an excellent substitute.

SPICY PEANUT DIP

MAKES ABOUT 500ml (¾ pint)

250g (8oz) peanut butter
2 garlic cloves, crushed
2.5cm (1in) piece fresh ginger, grated
juice of 1 lemon
4 tbsp soy sauce
2 tbsp runny honey
1 tsp turmeric
1 tsp Tabasco
125ml (4floz) water
salt, black pepper

Place peanut butter, garlic, ginger, lemon, soy sauce, honey, turmeric, Tabasco and water in a food processor or blender; pulse until smooth. If necessary, adjust consistency by gradually adding extra water 1 tbsp at a time. Add salt and pepper to taste. Cover and refrigerate for 30 minutes to allow the flavours to blend. Serve chilled.

THINK AHEAD
Make dip up to 3 days in advance. Cover and refrigerate.

SPICED ROAST AUBERGINE DIP

MAKES ABOUT 500ml (¾ pint)

2 medium aubergines, pricked
1 garlic clove, crushed
4 tbsp tahini
½ tsp ground cumin
1 tbsp lemon juice
125ml (4floz) Greek-style yoghurt
salt, cayenne pepper

Preheat oven to 200°C (400°F) Gas 6.
Place aubergine on an oven tray and roast until skin is black and blistered and flesh feels soft, 45 minutes. When cool enough to handle, peel off charred skin and squeeze out as much moisture as possible from the flesh.
Place aubergine and garlic in a food processor or blender; pulse until smooth. Add tahini, cumin, lemon and yoghurt; pulse to a smooth purée. Add salt and cayenne pepper to taste. Cover and refrigerate for 30 minutes to allow the flavours to blend. Serve chilled with dippers.

THINK AHEAD
Make dip up to 3 days in advance. Cover and refrigerate.

COOKS' NOTE
For an extra smoky flavour, grill the aubergines directly over a flame (either a barbecue or gas burner) until blackened on all sides. Peel and squeeze as directed.

TOPS AND BOTTOMS

TINY PARMESAN SHORTBREADS

MAKES 40

60g (2oz) plain flour, sifted
salt, cayenne pepper
45g (1½ oz) cold butter, diced
60g (2oz) parmesan cheese, grated

ESSENTIAL EQUIPMENT
3.5cm (1½ in) fluted pastry cutter,
baking parchment

Preheat oven to 180°C (350°F) Gas 4.
Place flour, a pinch each salt and
cayenne, butter, parmesan and any
additional flavouring, if using, in a
food processor; pulse to form a
smooth dough. Roll out dough on a
floured surface to a 0.5cm (¼ in)
thickness. Stamp out 40 rounds with
the pastry cutter. Place dough rounds
on parchment lined baking sheets
2cm (¾ in) apart and refrigerate for
30 minutes. Bake until golden brown,
8 minutes. Cool completely on a wire
rack before topping.

THINK AHEAD
Bake shortbreads up to 2 weeks in advance.
Store in an airtight container. Alternatively, bake
and freeze up to 1 month in advance. Defrost
and crisp in preheated 200°C (400°F) Gas 6 oven
for 3 minutes.

FLAVOURED VARIATIONS

PARMESAN AND ROSEMARY
SHORTBREADS
Add 1 tsp dried rosemary to the
ingredients.

PARMESAN AND BLACK OLIVE
SHORTBREADS
Add 1 tsp finely chopped black olives
to the ingredients.

TINY PARMESAN AND ROSEMARY SHORTBREADS WITH ROAST CHERRY TOMATOES AND FETA

MAKES 40

20 cherry tomatoes, halved
2 tsp olive oil
½ tsp runny honey
salt, black pepper
1 recipe tiny parmesan and rosemary
shortbreads (see opposite)
125g (4oz) feta cheese, crumbled
5 pitted black olives, quartered
rosemary leaves to garnish

Preheat oven 200°C (400°F) Gas 6.
Place tomato halves on an oven tray and
sprinkle with oil, honey, salt and pepper.
Roast in oven until softened, 20 minutes.
Top shortbreads with tomatoes and feta.
Garnish with olives and rosemary
leaves. Serve at room temperature.

THINK AHEAD
Prepare tomatoes up to 1 day in advance. Cover and
refrigerate. Bring to room temperature before using.
Top shortbreads up to 2 hours before serving.

TINY PARMESAN AND BLACK OLIVE SHORTBREADS WITH PARSLEY PESTO AND GOAT'S CHEESE

MAKES 40

15g (½ oz) parsley
2 tbsp pine nuts
4 tbsp parmesan cheese, grated
1 garlic clove, crushed
1 tbsp olive oil
salt, black pepper
1 recipe tiny parmesan and black olive
shortbreads (see opposite)
100g (3½ oz) fresh creamy goat's cheese
20 parsley leaves

Place parsley, pine nuts, parmesan,
garlic and oil in a food processor or
blender; pulse to a thick paste. Add salt
and pepper to taste. Use a teaspoon to
top shortbreads with pesto and goat's
cheese. Serve at room temperature.

THINK AHEAD
Make pesto up to 3 days in advance. Top
shortbreads up to 2 hours before serving.

COCKTAIL CORN CAKES
WITH SPICY MANGO SALSA

MAKES 20

FOR PANCAKES	FOR SALSA
3 tbsp medium cornmeal	½ mango, finely diced
60g (2oz) plain flour	(see page 163)
¼ tsp salt	½ medium red onion, finely
¼ tsp baking powder	chopped
1 egg, beaten	1 fresh green chilli, seeded and
5 tbsp milk	finely diced
1 tbsp melted butter	juice of 1 lime
125g (4oz) corn kernels	salt, black pepper
cayenne pepper	125ml (4floz) crème fraîche
1 tbsp sunflower oil	20 fresh coriander leaves

Mix the cornmeal, flour, salt, baking powder, egg, milk and butter to make a smooth batter. Stir in corn kernels. Add cayenne pepper to taste.

Brush a frying pan or griddle with oil. Preheat over medium heat. Working in batches, drop heaped teaspoonfuls of mixture into the hot pan. Cook until crisp and golden, 2½ minutes per side. Brush pan with more oil between each batch of pancakes. Cool pancakes to room temperature.

For salsa, combine mango, onion, chilli and lime. Add salt and pepper to taste. Top each cake with 1 teaspoonful each crème fraîche and salsa. Garnish with coriander leaves. Serve at room temperature.

THINK AHEAD
Make cakes up to 1 day in advance. Store in an airtight container in the refrigerator. Crisp in preheated 200°C (400°F) Gas 6 oven for 3 minutes. Make salsa up to 5 hours in advance. Cover and refrigerate. Top pancakes 45 minutes before serving.

COOKS' NOTE
The best flavour comes from fresh corn. Scrape kernels off the cob with a sharp knife. Use tinned corn, drained, frozen corn, defrosted, when fresh is not available.

WILD RICE AND SPRING ONION
PANCAKES WITH AVOCADO LIME SALSA

MAKES 20

FOR PANCAKES	FOR SALSA
4 tbsp wild rice	1 small avocado, finely diced
2 tbsp basmati rice	½ medium red onion, finely
60g (2oz) plain flour	chopped
¼ tsp salt	juice of 1 lime
1 egg, beaten	1 tbsp olive oil
4 tbsp milk	salt, Tabasco
2 tbsp spring onion, finely	2 spring onions, white stems only
chopped	
1 tbsp sunflower oil	

Cook each type of rice in a separate pot of boiling water until tender: wild rice, for 40 minutes; basmati rice, for 12 minutes. Drain and cool. Mix the flour, salt, egg and milk together to make a smooth batter. Stir both types of cooked rice and the chopped spring onions into the batter.

Brush a frying pan or griddle with oil. Preheat over medium heat. Working in batches, drop heaped teaspoonfuls of mixture into the hot pan. Cook until crisp and golden, 2½ minutes per side. Brush pan with additional oil between each batch of pancakes. Cool pancakes to room temperature.

For salsa, combine avocado, onion, lime and oil. Add salt and Tabasco to taste. For garnish, cut spring onions into 3.5cm (1½ in) pieces. Cut each piece into quarters lengthways. Top pancakes with equal amounts of salsa. Garnish each pancake with one piece of spring onion. Serve at room temperature.

THINK AHEAD
Make pancakes up to 1 day in advance. Store in an airtight container in the refrigerator. Crisp in preheated 200°C (400°F) Gas 6 oven, 3 minutes. Make salsa up to 2 hours in advance. Cover and refrigerate. Top pancakes 45 minutes before serving.

HERB PANCAKES

MAKES 20

60g (2oz) plain flour
¼ tsp baking powder
¼ tsp salt
1 egg, beaten
3 tbsp milk
1 tbsp finely chopped fresh herbs
1 tbsp sunflower oil

Sift flour, baking powder and salt together. Make a well in the centre. Add egg and milk to well. Gradually draw in flour and mix to a smooth batter. Stir in herbs (see below). Brush a frying pan or griddle with oil. Preheat over medium heat. Working in batches, drop heaped teaspoonfuls of mixture into the hot pan. Cook until bubbles appear and underside is golden, 3 minutes. Turn and brown other side, 2 minutes. Brush pan with more oil between each batch of pancakes. Cool pancakes. Serve at room temperature.

THINK AHEAD
Make pancakes up to 2 days in advance. Store in an airtight container in the refrigerator. Crisp in preheated 200°C (400°F) Gas 6 oven for 3 minutes.

VARIATIONS

DILL PANCAKES

Add 1 tbsp finely chopped dill to the ingredients.

CHIVE PANCAKES

Add 1 tbsp finely chopped chives to the ingredients.

DILL PANCAKES WITH SALMON CAVIAR AND LEMON CREME FRAICHE

MAKES 20

1 tsp grated lemon zest
1 tbsp lemon juice
125ml (4floz) crème fraîche
1 recipe dill pancakes (see above)
100g (3½oz) salmon caviar
20 dill sprigs to garnish

Mix lemon zest and juice into crème fraîche. Top each pancake with 1 teaspoonful each crème fraîche and salmon eggs. Garnish with dill. Serve at room temperature.

THINK AHEAD
Make lemon crème fraîche up to 1 day in advance. Cover and refrigerate. Top pancakes up to 45 minutes before serving.

CHIVE PANCAKES WITH CREME FRAICHE AND RED ONION CONFIT

MAKES 20

2 tbsp caster sugar
1 tbsp water
1 tbsp red wine vinegar
1 medium red onion, finely sliced
salt, black pepper
1 recipe chive pancakes (see opposite)
125ml (4floz) crème fraîche
1 tbsp finely chopped fresh chives

Put sugar and water in a small pan and stir to dissolve. Bring to boil over medium-low heat and cook to a dark caramel (see page 145). Remove from heat and add vinegar and onions. Return to medium heat and stir-fry until onions soften, 5 minutes. Add salt and pepper to taste. Cool to warm. Top each pancake with 1 teaspoonful each crème fraîche and onions. Garnish with chives. Serve at room temperature.

THINK AHEAD
Make onion confit up to 1 day in advance. Cover and store at room temperature. Top pancakes up to 45 minutes before serving.

BUCKWHEAT BLINIS WITH SOUR CREAM AND CAVIAR

MAKES 20

100g (3½oz) buckwheat flour
¼ tsp baking powder
¼ tsp salt
1 egg, separated
100ml (3½floz) milk
125ml (4floz) sour cream
100g (3½oz) caviar

Sift flour, baking powder and salt together. Make a well in the centre of the flour. Beat egg yolk and milk. Add to the well. Gradually draw flour into the egg mixture. Mix to a smooth batter. Whisk egg white until it holds soft peaks (see page 141). Gently fold the stiff egg white into the batter. Brush a frying pan or griddle with oil. Preheat over medium heat. Working in batches, drop heaped teaspoonfuls of mixture into the hot pan. Cook until bubbles appear and underside is golden, 3 minutes. Turn and brown other side, 2 minutes. Brush pan with oil between each batch of blinis. Cool blinis before topping. Top each blini with 1 teaspoonful each sour cream and caviar. Serve at room temperature.

THINK AHEAD
Make blinis up to 2 days in advance. Store in airtight container in refrigerator. Crisp in preheated 200°C (400°F) Gas 6 oven, 3 minutes. Top up to 30 minutes before serving.

CROSTINI

MAKES 20
20 slices day-old baguette, 1cm (½ in)
thick
4 tbsp olive oil

Preheat oven 180°C (350°F) Gas 4.
Place baguette slices on a baking
sheet. Brush with olive oil. Bake until
crisp and lightly golden, 10 minutes.
Serve plain or topped according to
the following recipes.

THINK AHEAD
Make crostini up to 2 weeks in advance. Cool
completely and store in an airtight container
at room temperature.

COOKS' NOTE
Choose a thin baguette about 5–8cm (2–3in) in
diameter. Add a crushed clove of garlic to the oil
before brushing the bread for extra flavour.

SPICY PRAWN CROSTINI

MAKES 20
200g (7oz) medium prawns
½ medium red onion, finely chopped
1 garlic clove, crushed
½ tsp crushed chilli flakes
2 tbsp olive oil
1 tbsp lemon juice
salt, black pepper
1 tbsp finely chopped parsley
1 recipe crostini (see opposite)

Combine prawns with onion, garlic,
chilli, oil and lemon. Add salt and
pepper to taste and stir in parsley.
Spoon on to crostini. Serve at
room temperature.

THINK AHEAD
Make topping up to 1 day in advance, but add salt,
pepper and parsley just before serving for the best
texture and colour. Store in an airtight container in
the refrigerator. Top crostini up to 1 hour before
serving.

TOMATO AND BASIL CROSTINI

MAKES 20
5 ripe plum tomatoes, seeded and diced
(see page 147)
½ medium red onion, finely chopped
1 garlic clove, crushed
2 tbsp olive oil
1 tbsp balsamic vinegar
salt, black pepper
1 recipe crostini (see opposite)
20 tiny basil sprigs to garnish

Mix tomato, onion, garlic, oil and
vinegar together. Add salt and pepper to
taste. Spoon on to crostini. Garnish with
basil sprigs. Serve at room temperature.

THINK AHEAD
Make topping up to 1 day in advance, but add the
salt and pepper just before serving. Store in an
airtight container in the refrigerator. Top crostini up
to 45 minutes before serving.

COOKS' NOTE
Basil is the tomato's classic culinary partner. Try
rocket in place of basil for a deep, peppery bite. Stir
in a handful of sliced rocket just before serving.
Reserve some smaller leaves for the garnish.

WHITE BEAN AND SAGE CROSTINI

MAKES 20
3 tbsp olive oil
1 small onion, finely chopped
2 garlic cloves, finely chopped
4 sage leaves, finely chopped
400g (14oz) tinned cannellini beans, drained
2 tbsp water
salt, black pepper
1 recipe crostini (see page 42)
1 seeded ripe tomato, diced (see page 147)
extra olive oil for drizzling

Heat oil in a saucepan. Add onion, garlic and sage and cook over a low heat until soft, about 5 minutes. Add beans, water and salt and pepper to taste. Cook for about 10 minutes. Mash the beans with a wooden spoon to make a rough purée. Spread bean purée on crostini. Top each crostini with a little tomato dice and a drizzle of olive oil. Serve warm or at room temperature.

THINK AHEAD
Make topping up to 3 days in advance. Cover and refrigerate. Return to room temperature before serving. Top crostini up to 1 hour before serving.

AUBERGINE CAVIAR CROSTINI

MAKES 20
2 medium aubergines, pricked with a fork
1 garlic clove, crushed
juice of ½ lemon
2 tbsp olive oil
1 tbsp Greek-style yoghurt
salt, cayenne pepper
1 recipe crostini (see page 42)
20 mint sprigs
1 tsp paprika

Grill aubergine until skin is black and blistered, and the flesh feels soft. When cool enough to handle, peel off charred skin. Use hands to squeeze out as much moisture as possible from the flesh. Place aubergine, garlic, lemon, oil and yoghurt in a food processor or blender; pulse to a smooth purée. Add salt and cayenne pepper to taste. Cool completely. Spoon topping on to each crostini. Garnish with mint sprigs and a pinch of paprika. Serve at room temperature.

THINK AHEAD
Make topping up to 2 days in advance. Cover and refrigerate. Top crostini up to 45 minutes before serving.

AVOCADO AND GOAT'S CHEESE CROSTINI

MAKES 20
1 large avocado
150g (5oz) fresh creamy goat's cheese
grated zest and juice of 1 lemon
1 tbsp olive oil
salt, Tabasco
1 recipe crostini (see page 42)

Place avocado, cheese, zest, juice and oil in a food processor or blender; pulse to a smooth purée. Add salt and Tabasco to taste. Spoon topping on to each crostini. Serve at room temperature.

THINK AHEAD
Make topping up to 6 hours in advance. Store in a bowl with cling film, pressing directly on to purée to prevent contact with air. This will prevent discoloration. Keep refrigerated and stir before using. Top crostini up to 20 minutes before serving.

MINI MANGO GALETTES

MAKES 20

200g (7oz) puff pastry
200g (7oz) tin of sliced mangoes, drained
2 tbsp apricot jam
2 tsp icing sugar for dusting

Preheat oven to 200°C (400°F) Gas 6. Roll out pastry on a floured surface to a 0.25cm (⅛in) thickness. Cut pastry into approximately 20 squares, measuring 5cm x 5cm (2in x 2in) each. Trace a fine line inside each square using a sharp knife (see below, left). Take care not to actually cut through the pastry. Prick the centre of each pastry square with a fork (see below, right). Place pastry squares on a floured baking sheet. Cut mango slices across into 0.5cm (¼in) thick slices. Arrange 2 or 3 mango pieces, slightly overlapping, on top of each pastry square. Bake until pastry is crisp and golden, 10 minutes. Melt apricot jam with 1 tbsp water over low heat to make glaze. Allow galettes to cool, then brush with apricot glaze. Dust with icing sugar. Serve at room temperature.

THINK AHEAD
Same as mini apple galettes.

Trace a fine line using a sharp knife.

Prick centre with a fork.

MINI APPLE GALETTES

MAKES 20

200g (7oz) puff pastry
2 apples, quartered and cored
2 tbsp apricot jam
2 tsp icing sugar for dusting

ESSENTIAL EQUIPMENT
5cm (2in) plain pastry cutter

Preheat oven to 200°C (400°F) Gas 6. Roll out pastry on a floured surface to a 0.25cm (⅛in) thickness. Stamp out 20 rounds with the pastry cutter. Place rounds on to a floured baking sheet. Cut each apple quarter across into fine slices. Arrange apple slices, slightly overlapping, on each pastry round. Bake until pastry is crisp and golden, 10 minutes. Melt apricot jam with 1 tbsp water over low heat to make glaze. Allow galettes to cool, then brush with apricot glaze. Dust with icing sugar. Serve at room temperature.

THINK AHEAD
Assemble and bake up to 1 day in advance. Store in an airtight container at room temperature. Glaze up to 5 hours in advance.

MINI CHERRY TOMATO AND BASIL PESTO GALETTES

MAKES 20

15g (½oz) basil
2 tbsp pine nuts
1 tbsp olive oil
4 tbsp parmesan cheese, grated
200g (7oz) puff pastry
20 cherry tomatoes, each cut into 3 slices
salt, black pepper
20 basil sprigs to garnish

ESSENTIAL EQUIPMENT
5cm (2in) fluted pastry cutter

For pesto, place basil, pine nuts, oil and parmesan in a food processor or blender; pulse to a thick paste. Preheat oven to 200°C (400°F) Gas 6. Roll out pastry on a floured surface to a 0.25cm (⅛in) thickness. Stamp out 20 rounds with the pastry cutter. Place pastry rounds on to a floured baking sheet. Spread ½ tsp pesto on to each pastry round and top with 3 cherry tomato slices. Sprinkle with salt and pepper. Bake until crisp and golden, 10 minutes. Garnish each galette with ½ tsp pesto and a basil sprig. Serve warm.

THINK AHEAD
Make pesto up to 3 days in advance. Cover and refrigerate. Bake galettes up to 1 day in advance. Reheat in a preheated 200°C (400°F) Gas 6 oven for 3 minutes. Garnish and serve warm.

ROAST RED ONION AND THYME FOCACCINE

MAKES 20

**1 recipe unbaked bread dough
(see page 140)**
125g (4oz) gruyère cheese, grated
1 medium red onion, quartered
coarse salt, black pepper
3 thyme sprigs, roughly chopped

ESSENTIAL EQUIPMENT
5cm (2in) plain pastry cutter

Preheat oven to 200°C (400°F) Gas 6.
Roll out dough on a floured surface
to a 0.5cm (¼in) thickness. Stamp out
20 rounds with the pastry cutter. Place
on to a floured baking sheet and
sprinkle with cheese. Cut each onion
quarter across into 5 slices. Place a slice
on top of each round. Sprinkle with salt,
pepper and thyme. Bake until crisp and
golden, 15 minutes. Serve warm.

THINK AHEAD
Bake up to 1 day in advance. Store in an airtight
container at room temperature. Crisp in a preheated
200°C (400°F) Gas 6 oven for 10 minutes.
Alternatively, assemble and freeze unbaked for up
to 1 month (see page 149). Bake from frozen in
preheated 200°C (400°F) Gas 6 oven for 20 minutes.

POTATO AND ROSEMARY FOCACCINE

MAKES 20

20 (about 500g (1lb)) baby new potatoes
**1 recipe unbaked bread dough
(see page 140)**
125g (4oz) gruyère cheese, grated
½ tsp salt, ¼ tsp black pepper
**3 rosemary sprigs, separated into 20 pieces
(see page 147)**

ESSENTIAL EQUIPMENT
5cm (2in) plain pastry cutter

Preheat oven to 200°C (400°F) Gas 6.
Cut potatoes into 0.5cm (¼in) thick
slices. Place potato slices in boiling
water and cook for 5 minutes from the
time the water has returned to a boil.
Drain and cool. Roll out dough on a
floured surface to a 0.5cm (¼in)
thickness. Stamp out 20 rounds with
the pastry cutter. Place on to a floured
baking sheet. Sprinkle all the rounds
evenly with about three quarters of the
cheese. Arrange 4 potato slices on top of
each round. Sprinkle over the remaining
cheese and salt and pepper. Top each
round with a tuft of rosemary. Bake until
crisp and golden, 15 minutes. Serve warm.

THINK AHEAD
Bake up to 1 day in advance. Store in an airtight
container at room temperature. Crisp in a preheated
200°C (400°F) Gas 6 oven for 10 minutes.
Alternatively, assemble and freeze unbaked for up
to 1 month (see page 149). Bake from frozen in
preheated 200°C (400°F) Gas 6 oven for 20 minutes.

ARTICHOKE AND GORGONZOLA FOCACCINE

MAKES 20

**1 recipe unbaked bread dough
(see page 140)**
**125g (4oz) gorgonzola or Danish blue
cheese, crumbled**
salt, black pepper
**20 baby artichokes hearts in oil, drained
and halved**
2 tbsp oregano leaves

ESSENTIAL EQUIPMENT
5cm (2in) plain pastry cutter

Preheat oven to 200°C (400°F) Gas 6.
Roll out dough on a floured surface
to a 0.5cm (¼in) thickness. Stamp out
20 rounds with the pastry cutter. Place
on to a floured baking sheet. Sprinkle
each round with cheese, salt and pepper.
Top with 2 artichoke halves. Bake until
crisp and golden, 15 minutes. Garnish
with oregano leaves and serve warm.

THINK AHEAD
Bake up to 1 day in advance. Store in an airtight
container at room temperature. Crisp in a preheated
200°C (400°F) Gas 6 oven for 10 minutes.
Alternatively, assemble and freeze unbaked for up
1 month (see page 149). Bake from frozen in
preheated 200°C (400°F) Gas 6 oven for 20 minutes.

CROUTES

MAKES 20

7 medium slices white bread

ESSENTIAL EQUIPMENT
5cm (2in) fluted pastry cutter

Preheat oven to 150°C
(300°F) Gas 2.

Stamp out each slice into
3 rounds. Place on a baking
sheet and bake until crisp,
25 minutes. Cool.

THINK AHEAD
Make up to 3 days in advance.
Store in an airtight container at
room temperature.

GRILLED BEEF FILLET WITH SALSA VERDE CROUTES

MAKES 20
15g (½ oz) parsley
10 basil leaves
10 mint leaves
1 garlic clove, crushed
1 tbsp creamy Dijon mustard
1 tbsp drained capers
2 drained anchovy fillets
2 tbsp olive oil
salt, black pepper
350g (12oz) beef fillet steak, 1.5cm (¾ in) thick
1 recipe croutes (see above)

ESSENTIAL EQUIPMENT
2.5cm (1½ in) plain pastry cutter, cast-iron grill pan

For salsa, place fresh herbs, garlic, mustard, capers, anchovies
and oil in a food processor or blender; pulse to a thick paste.
Add salt and pepper to taste. Stamp steak into 20 rounds with
a pastry cutter (see below). Preheat grill pan over high heat.
Sear steak rounds, about 3 minutes per side. Sprinkle with salt
and pepper. Place one round on to each croute. Top with salsa.
Serve warm or at room temperature.

FRESH SALMON TARTARE CROUTES

MAKES 20
250g (8oz) fresh salmon fillet
juice of 1 lemon
2 tbsp drained cornichons, finely chopped
2 tbsp drained capers, finely chopped
1 tbsp mayonnaise (see page 142)
1 tsp grainy mustard
1 tbsp finely chopped tarragon
½ tsp salt
½ tsp Tabasco
½ lemon, peeled (see page 147)
1 recipe croutes (see above)

Cut salmon into fine dice and place in a bowl. Toss salmon
pieces with lemon juice to coat. Cover and refrigerate for
3 hours. Drain off lemon juice and discard. Add cornichons,
capers, mayonnaise, mustard, tarragon and salt to salmon.
Stir to coat. Add Tabasco to taste. Cut lemon into segment
wedges (see below). Spoon salmon tartare on to croutes.
Garnish with lemon wedges. Served chilled.

THINK AHEAD
Prepare topping up to 1 day in advance. Cover and refrigerate. Top croutes up to
30 minutes in advance. Garnish and serve chilled.

**STAMPING OUT
STEAK ROUNDS**

LEMON SEGMENTS
Cut lemon half into 4 slices.

Cut each slice into wedges.

GRIDDLED SCALLOPS WITH SWEET CHILLI SAUCE AND CREME FRAICHE

MAKES 20

10 sea scallops
salt, black pepper
4 tbsp Thai sweet chilli sauce
1 recipe croutes (see page 46)
6 tbsp crème fraîche
20 coriander leaves to garnish

ESSENTIAL EQUIPMENT
cast-iron grill pan

Cut each scallop in half. Preheat grill pan over high heat. Sear scallops, 1 minute per side. Sprinkle with salt and pepper to taste and toss with chilli sauce. Place 1 scallop half on to each croute. Top with 1 tsp crème fraîche. Garnish with coriander leaves. Serve at room temperature or chilled.

THINK AHEAD
Sear and sauce scallops up to 1 day in advance. Cover and refrigerate. Top croutes up to 1 hour in advance.

COOKS' NOTE
Barbecue scallops for best flavour. Place on an oiled rack set 8cm (3in) above medium hot coals. Cook 1 minute per side.

SEARED TUNA NICOISE CROUTES

MAKES 20

200g (7oz) tuna steak, 2.5cm (1in) thick
salt, black pepper
½ romaine heart, leaves separated
10 green beans
1 tomato, seeded and diced (see page 147)
2 tbsp drained baby capers
10 anchovy fillets, roughly chopped
10 pitted black olives, sliced
2 tbsp olive oil
1 tbsp red wine vinegar
salt, black pepper
1 recipe croutes (see page 46)
2 tbsp mayonnaise (see page 142)

ESSENTIAL EQUIPMENT
cast-iron grill pan.

Cut tuna into 2.5cm (1in) cubes. Preheat grill pan over high heat. Sear tuna cubes on both sides until firm to the touch, 2 minutes per side. Season with salt and pepper. Cool. Cut stalks from salad leaves and discard. Cut each leaf into 2.5cm (1in) pieces. Cut beans into 1cm (½in) lengths. Put beans in to a pan of boiling water. Once the water returns to a boil, drain beans and refresh in cold water. Pat dry with kitchen paper. Toss beans, tomato, capers, anchovies and olives with oil and vinegar. Add salt and pepper to taste. Spread each croute with mayonnaise and top with a salad leaf. Place tuna on top. Garnish with vegetables. Serve at room temperature.

THINK AHEAD
Prepare vegetables up to 1 day in advance. Cover and refrigerate. Cook tuna up to 2 hours in advance. Keep at room temperature until ready to assemble. Top croutes up to 1 hour in advance.

ASPARAGUS CROUTES WITH LEMON HOLLANDAISE

MAKES 20

10 medium asparagus tips, halved lengthwise
15g (½oz) chives
1 recipe lemon hollandaise (see page 143)
1 recipe croutes (see page 46)
1 tsp paprika to dust

Put asparagus in to a pan of boiling water. Once the water returns to a boil, drain asparagus and refresh immediately in cold water. Pat dry with kitchen paper. Cut chives on the diagonal into 2.5cm (1in) lengths. Spoon hollandaise on to croutes and top with asparagus halves. Dust with paprika. Garnish with chives. Serve at room temperature.

THINK AHEAD
Cook asparagus up to 1 day in advance. Cover and refrigerate. Top croutes up to 1 hour in advance.

TINY SCONES

MAKES 10

175g (6oz) plain flour
1½ tsp baking powder
pinch of salt
45g (1½oz) butter, diced
1½ tbsp caster sugar
1 egg, beaten
60ml (2floz) cream

ESSENTIAL EQUIPMENT
4cm (1½in) fluted pastry cutter
Preheat oven to 200°C (400°F) Gas 6.

Sift flour, baking powder, and salt. Crumble the butter into the flour with fingers until mixture resembles fine crumbs. Stir in sugar (omit if making savoury scones) and any additional flavouring, if using. With a fork, stir in egg and enough cream to make a soft dough. Turn dough on to a floured surface and knead lightly until smooth. Gently roll out to a 2.5cm (1in) thickness and stamp out 10 rounds with the pastry cutter. Place rounds on a greased and floured baking sheet. Bake until firm and golden, 8–10 minutes. Cool on a wire rack.

VARIATIONS

TINY DILL SCONES
Replace sugar with 1 tbsp finely chopped dill.

TINY HEART-SHAPED SCONES
Stamp out dough with a 6cm (2½in) heart-shaped pastry cutter.

THINK AHEAD
Bake scones up to 1 week in advance. Store in an airtight container at room temperature.

COOKS' NOTE
Cover the scones with a cloth as they cool on the wire rack. This will keep some of the steam in, making the scones perfectly soft, moist and light.

TINY DILL SCONES WITH SMOKED TROUT AND HORSERADISH CREAM

MAKES 20

1 recipe tiny dill scones (see above)
125ml (4floz) sour cream
1 tbsp horseradish sauce
150g (5oz) smoked trout slices
black pepper
20 tiny dill sprigs to garnish

Cut each scone in half. Combine cream and horseradish sauce. Top each scone half with an equal amount of mixture. Cut smoked trout slices into 20 - 2.5cm (1in) wide strips. Top each prepared half with a smoked trout strip and a sprinkle of pepper. Garnish with dill sprigs. Serve at room temperature.

THINK AHEAD
Top scones up to 45 minutes in advance. Garnish just before serving.

TINY DEVONSHIRE CREAM TEA SCONES WITH RASPBERRY CONSERVE

MAKES 20

1 recipe tiny scones (see above)
125ml (4floz) raspberry conserve
125ml (4floz) double cream

Cut each scone in half. Whip cream until it holds soft peaks (see page 144). Top each scone half with 1 tsp each conserve and cream. Serve at room temperature.

THINK AHEAD
Top scones up to 30 minutes in advance.

TINY HEART SHORTCAKES WITH STRAWBERRIES

MAKES 20

1 recipe heart-shaped tiny scones (see above)
125ml (4floz) double cream
2 tbsp caster sugar
10 strawberries, halved
2 tsp icing sugar for dusting

ESSENTIAL EQUIPMENT
Piping bag with a large star nozzle

Cut each scone in half. Whip cream until it holds stiff peaks. Whisk in caster sugar (see page 144). Fill piping bag with cream. Pipe 3 small rosettes on to each scone half (see page 146). Arrange strawberry on top. Dust with icing sugar. Serve at room temperature.

THINK AHEAD
Top scones up to 30 minutes in advance.

MINI PISSALADIERE

MAKES 24

1 recipe unbaked shortcrust pastry
(see page 136)
1 tbsp olive oil
1 garlic clove, crushed
2 large Spanish onions, finely sliced
200ml (7floz) tomato passata
1 tsp dried oregano
salt, black pepper
1 tbsp parmesan cheese, grated
24 pitted black olives
6 anchovies, halved lengthways

ESSENTIAL EQUIPMENT
35cm x 25cm (14in x 10in) Swiss roll pan

Preheat oven to 200°C (400°F) Gas 6.
Roll out pastry on a floured surface to
fit pan. Place rolled pastry in an oiled
pan. Heat oil in a frying pan over
medium heat. Add garlic and onion and
cook until soft, 10 minutes. Add tomato
passata and continue cooking for
5 minutes. Add oregano, and salt and
pepper to taste. Spread onion mixture
evenly over pastry. Bake for 15 minutes.
Remove from oven and sprinkle with
parmesan. Allow to cool in pan then cut
into 24 squares, 5cm x 5cm (2in x 2in).
Cut anchovy pieces in half crosswise.
Top each square with 2 anchovy pieces
in a criss-cross pattern with an olive in
the centre. Remove from pan and serve
at room temperature.

THINK AHEAD
Make, cut and garnish, but leave in pan, up to 2 days
in advance. Store in pan covered in the refrigerator.
Crisp in preheated 200°C (400°F) Gas 6 oven for 10
minutes. Remove from pan before serving.

AUBERGINE AND PINE NUT PIZZETTE

MAKES 20

1 recipe unbaked bread dough
(see page 140)
1 medium aubergine
1 tbsp olive oil
1 garlic clove, crushed
2 tbsp finely chopped parsley
125ml (4floz) tomato passata
4 tbsp parmesan cheese, grated
3 tbsp pine nuts
salt, black pepper

ESSENTIAL EQUIPMENT
5cm (2in) plain pastry cutter

Preheat oven to 200°C (400°F) Gas 6.
Roll out dough on a floured surface
to a 0.25cm (⅛in) thickness. Stamp out
20 rounds with the pastry cutter and
place on a floured baking sheet.
Cut aubergine in half lengthwise, then
cut halves into 0.5cm (¼in) thick slices.
Heat oil in a frying pan and add
aubergine, garlic and parsley. Stir-fry
over high heat until wilted, 5 minutes.
Spread each pizzette with 1 tsp tomato
passata. Arrange aubergine slices on
top. Sprinkle with parmesan, pine nuts,
salt and pepper. Bake until crisp and
golden, 10 minutes. Serve warm.

THINK AHEAD
Make up to 1 day in advance. Cover and refrigerate.
Crisp in preheated 200°C (400°F) Gas 6 oven for
10 minutes before serving.

TOMATO AND BASIL PIZZETTE

MAKES 20

1 recipe unbaked bread dough
(see page 140)
125g (4oz) mozzarella cheese, finely sliced
125ml (4floz) tomato passata
15g (½oz) small basil leaves
4 tbsp parmesan cheese, grated
salt, black pepper

ESSENTIAL EQUIPMENT
5cm (2in) plain pastry cutter

Preheat oven to 200°C (400°F) Gas 6.
Roll dough out on a floured surface to
a 0.25cm (⅛in) thickness. Stamp out
20 rounds with the pastry cutter and
place on a floured baking sheet.
Cut mozzarella slices into 20 equal-sized
pieces. Spread each round with 1 tsp
tomato passata and arrange over 2 basil
leaves. Place a piece of mozzarella on
top. Sprinkle with parmesan, salt and
pepper. Bake until crisp and golden,
10 minutes. Serve warm.

THINK AHEAD
Make up to 1 day in advance. Cover and refrigerate.
Crisp in preheated 200°C (400°F) Gas 6 oven for
10 minutes before serving.

MINI APPLE TATINS

MAKES 20

100g (3½ oz) puff pastry
100g (3½ oz) caster sugar
2 tbsp water
2½ apples, quartered and cored
2 tsp icing sugar for dusting

ESSENTIAL EQUIPMENT
2 - 12 cup bun tins or 2 -12 cup mini muffin tins, 5cm (2in) plain pastry cutter

Preheat oven 200°C (400°F) Gas 6. Roll out pastry on a floured surface to a 0.5cm (¼in) thickness. Stamp out 20 rounds with the pastry cutter.
Put sugar and water in a small pan. Stir to dissolve, then place over medium heat and bring to boil. Cook to a dark caramel (see page 145). Divide caramel evenly among 20 of the bun or muffin cups.
Cut each apple quarter across into 6 slices, about 0.5cm (¼in) thick. Arrange 3 apple pieces over the caramel in each cup. Press pastry rounds on top. Bake until pastry is crisp and golden, 10 minutes. Cool slightly before turning out. Dust with icing sugar. Serve warm.

THINK AHEAD
Bake up to 1 day in advance, but do not turn out of tins. Store covered at room temperature. Reheat in preheated 200°C (400°F) Gas 6 oven for 10 minutes. Finish as directed.

COOKS' NOTE
In France, Golden Delicious apples are traditionally used for making tarte tatin. This is because they retain their shape well and do not disintegrate when baked. Granny Smith or Cox apples, however, also give good results.

MINI RED ONION TATINS

MAKES 20

2 red onions
2 tsp finely chopped thyme
salt, black pepper
1 tbsp olive oil
100g (3½ oz) puff pastry
100g (3½ oz) caster sugar
2 tbsp water
1 tbsp balsamic vinegar
3 thyme sprigs, roughly chopped, to garnish

ESSENTIAL EQUIPMENT
2 - 12-cup bun tins or 2 - 12-cup mini muffin tin, 5cm (2in) plain pastry cutter

Preheat oven to 200°C (400°F) Gas 6. Cut each onion quarter across into 5 pieces, about 0.5cm (¼in) each. Place pieces on an oiled baking sheet. Sprinkle with chopped thyme, salt, pepper and oil. Bake for 10 minutes.
Meanwhile, roll out pastry on a floured surface to a 0.5cm (¼in) thickness. Stamp out 20 rounds with the pastry cutter. Put sugar and water in a small pan and stir to dissolve. Place over medium heat and bring to a boil. Cook to a dark caramel (see page 145). Divide caramel evenly among 20 of the muffin cups. Arrange 2 onion pieces over the caramel in each muffin cup. Press pastry rounds on top. Bake until pastry is crisp and golden, 10 minutes. Cool slightly before turning out. Sprinkle with thyme and drizzle with vinegar. Serve warm.

THINK AHEAD
Bake up to 1 day in advance, but do not turn out of tins. Store covered at room temperature. Reheat in preheated 200°C (400°F) Gas 6 oven for 5 minutes. Turn out and finish as directed.

CANAPES

MAKES 20

7 thin slices bread

SPECIAL EQUIPMENT

5cm (2in) fluted pastry cutter

Stamp bread slices into 20 rounds with the pastry cutter.

THINK AHEAD

Prepare up to 1 day in advance. Store in an airtight container.

COOKS' NOTE

We urge you to look beyond white and brown bread for canapé bases; the wealth of speciality breads now available offer a short-cut to simple but flavoursome canapés. Also try using different shaped cutters – another easy but sure-fire way to add instant appeal.

GRAVLAX ON PUMPERNICKEL CANAPES WITH DILL-MUSTARD SAUCE

MAKES 20

1½ tsp white wine vinegar

2 tsp sugar

2 tbsp creamy Dijon mustard

1 tbsp finely chopped dill

1 tsp white pepper

2½ tbsp sunflower oil

300g (10oz) gravlax slices

5 pumpernickel slices

For sauce, combine vinegar, sugar, mustard, dill and pepper; whisk in oil until thick and creamy. Lay gravlax on the pumpernickel slices. Cut each pumpernickel and gravlax slice into 20 - 2.5cm (1in) wide strips. Drizzle with sauce. Serve chilled or at room temperature. Garnish with more dill.

THINK AHEAD

Assemble up to 3 hours in advance. Cover tightly with cling film and refrigerate. Drizzle with sauce up to 1 hour before serving.

VALENTINE CUCUMBER CREAM CANAPES

MAKES 20

½ cucumber

200g (7oz) cream cheese

10 thin white bread slices

3 tbsp finely chopped parsley

salt, white pepper

ESSENTIAL EQUIPMENT

3.5cm (1½ in) heart-shaped pastry cutter

6cm (2½ in) heart-shaped pastry cutter

Cut cucumber into 0.5cm (¼in) slices. Stamp out 20 cucumber hearts with smaller cutter. Spread cream cheese on bread. Stamp out 20 canapé hearts with larger pastry cutter. Put parsley on small dish. Dip edges of canapés in parsley. Top canapés with cucumber hearts and sprinkle with salt and pepper. Serve chilled or at room temperature.

THINK AHEAD

Assemble up to 3 hours in advance. Cover tightly with cling film and refrigerate.

SMOKED OYSTERS ON RYE CANAPES WITH SOUR CREAM AND TARRAGON

MAKES 20
20 drained smoked oysters
150ml (5floz) sour cream
1 recipe rye canapé bases (see page 52)
salt, black pepper
20 tarragon sprigs to garnish

Pat oysters dry with kitchen paper. Divide sour cream evenly among canapé bases. Place oyster on top and sprinkle with salt and pepper. Garnish with tarragon. Serve chilled or at room temperature.

THINK AHEAD
Top canapés up to 45 minutes in advance.

PARIS HAM WITH DIJON BUTTER CANAPES

MAKES 20
90g (3oz) butter, softened
1 tsp creamy Dijon mustard
1 recipe white bread canapé bases (see page 52)
200g (7oz) ham, thickly sliced
20 cornichon fans to garnish (see below)

ESSENTIAL EQUIPMENT
5cm (2in) fluted pastry cutter

Mix butter and mustard. Spread on canapé bases. Stamp out 20 rounds of ham with pastry cutter. Fold each ham round in half and place on canapés. Garnish with cornichon fans. Serve chilled or at room temperature.

THINK AHEAD
Top canapés up to 3 hours in advance. Cover tightly with cling film and refrigerate.

CARPACCIO CANAPES

MAKES 20
1 tbsp mayonnaise (see page 142)
dash of Worcestershire sauce
squeeze of lemon juice
1 tbsp milk
salt, white pepper
100g (3½ oz) beef fillet steak, 2.5cm (1in) thick
1 recipe brown bread canapé bases (see page 52)

ESSENTIAL EQUIPMENT
paper piping cone (see page 146)

Combine mayonnaise, Worcestershire sauce, lemon and milk. Add salt and pepper to taste. Cut steak across the grain into 5cm (2in) wide strips. Place strips end to end in a line on top of a piece of foil. Roll beef strips up tightly in the foil. Twist the ends of foil to give the beef strips a rounded shape. Chill for 20 minutes in freezer. Cut beef into 2.5mm (⅛in) slices (see below, left). Flatten each slice by setting the blade of the knife on top and pressing down lightly. Divide beef slices among canapé bases. Fill paper piping cone with sauce. Pipe over sauce. Serve at room temperature.

THINK AHEAD
Make sauce up to 1 day in advance. Cover and refrigerate. Roll beef up to 1 day in advance; refrigerate. Top canapés up to 45 minutes in advance.

COOKS' NOTE
If you don't feel comfortable serving raw beef, rare roast beef slices can be used as an alternative. Use a 5cm (2in) pastry cutter to cut the roast beef into rounds. Top canapés and drizzle over sauce.

CORNICHON FANS
Cut 10 cornichons in half lengthwise. Cut fine slices through each cornichon half, leaving slices attached at one end.

BEETROOT ROSTI WITH SMOKED TROUT AND HORSERADISH MOUSSE

MAKES 20

FOR MOUSSE
150g (5oz) smoked trout
125g (4oz) cream cheese
1 tbsp horseradish sauce
1 tbsp lemon juice
cayenne pepper

ESSENTIAL EQUIPMENT
23cm (9in) non-stick frying pan, 4.5cm (1¾ in) fluted pastry cutter, piping bag with a large star nozzle

FOR ROSTI
250g (8oz) cooked beetroot, grated
250g (8oz) potatoes, grated and squeezed dry
1 tbsp plain flour
1 egg, beaten
¾ tsp salt, ¼ tsp black pepper
2 tbsp sunflower oil
paprika to garnish

For mousse, place trout, cream cheese, horseradish and lemon in a food processor or blender; pulse to a smooth paste. Add cayenne pepper to taste.
For rosti, mix beetroot, potato, flour, egg, salt and pepper together. Heat 1 tbsp oil in the non-stick pan. Spread half the potato mixture, 0.5cm (¼in) thick, across the bottom of the pan. Reduce heat to low and cook until both sides are crisp and golden, about 10 minutes per side. Remove from pan and cool slightly on kitchen paper. Heat the remaining oil. Cook and cool the remaining potato mixture. Stamp out 10 rounds from each rosti with the pastry cutter (see opposite, middle). Cool completely before topping. Fill piping bag with mousse and pipe on to rostis (see page 146). Sprinkle with paprika to garnish. Serve at room temperature.

THINK AHEAD
Make mousse up to 3 days in advance. Cover and refrigerate. Make rosti rounds up to 2 days in advance. Store in layers on greaseproof paper in an airtight container in the refrigerator. Crisp in preheated 200°C (400°F) Gas 6 oven for 5 minutes. Top and garnish up to 1 hour before serving.

Stamp out rounds from each rosti.

POTATO ROSTI WITH CREME FRAICHE, CAVIAR AND DILL

MAKES 20

500g (1lb) potatoes, grated and squeezed dry
1 tsp flour
¾ tsp salt, ¼ tsp black pepper
2 tbsp sunflower oil
125ml (4floz) crème fraîche
100g (3½oz) black lumpfish caviar
20 dill sprigs to garnish

ESSENTIAL EQUIPMENT
23cm (9in) non-stick frying pan, 4.5cm (1¾ in) plain pastry cutter

Mix potato, flour, salt and pepper together. Heat 1 tbsp oil in the non-stick pan. Spread half the potato mixture, 0.5cm (¼in) thick, across the bottom of the pan. Reduce heat to low and cook until both sides are crisp and golden, about 10 minutes per side. Remove from pan and cool slightly on paper towels. Heat the remaining oil. Cook and cool the remaining potato mixture.
Stamp out 10 rounds from each rosti with the pastry cutter (see opposite, middle). Cool completely before topping. Top mini rostis with 1 tsp each crème fraîche and caviar. Garnish with dill sprigs. Serve warm.

THINK AHEAD
Make rosti rounds up to 2 days in advance. Store in layers on greaseproof paper in an airtight container in the refrigerator. Crisp in preheated 200°C (400°F) Gas 6 oven for 5 minutes. Top up to 45 minutes before serving.

MINI LATKES WITH SOUR CREAM AND APPLE SAUCE

MAKES 20

500g (1lb) potatoes, grated
and squeezed dry
1 onion, grated and squeezed dry
1 tbsp plain flour
1 egg, beaten
¾ tsp salt, ¼ tsp black pepper
2 tbsp sunflower oil
125ml (4floz) sour cream
125ml (4floz) apple sauce
2 tbsp finely chopped chives

Mix potatoes, onion, flour, egg, salt and
pepper together. Heat oil in a frying pan
over medium heat. Working in batches,
drop heaped teaspoonfuls of mixture
into the hot oil. Use the back of spoon
to flatten them into thin pancakes.
Cook, turning once, until crisp and
golden on each side. Drain on kitchen
paper. Cool slightly before topping.
Top latkes with 1 tsp each sour cream
and apple sauce. Garnish with chopped
chives. Serve warm or at room
temperature.

THINK AHEAD
Make latkes up to 2 days in advance. Store in layers
on greaseproof paper in an airtight container in the
refrigerator. Crisp in preheated 200°C (400°F) Gas 6
oven for 5 minutes. Top up to 45 minutes before
serving.

COOKS' NOTE
The oaky, salty flavour of smoked fish perfectly
complements these crispy potato pancakes. Try the
classic combination of smoked salmon, sour cream,
and a squeeze of lemon.

CRISPY CARROT AND SPRING ONION CAKES WITH FETA AND BLACK OLIVE

MAKES 20

250g (8oz) carrots, grated
250g (8oz) potatoes, grated and
squeezed dry
2 spring onions, finely chopped
1 tbsp plain flour
1 egg, beaten
¾ tsp salt, ¼ tsp black pepper
2 tbsp sunflower oil
100g (3½ oz) feta cheese, crumbled
10 pitted black olives, quartered

Mix carrot, potato, spring onion, flour,
egg and salt and pepper together. Heat
oil in a frying pan over medium heat.
Working in batches, drop heaped
teaspoonfuls of mixture into the hot oil.
Use the back of the spoon to flatten
them into thin pancakes. Cook, turning
once, until crisp and golden on each
side, 5 minutes per side. Drain on paper
towels. Cool to room temperature before
topping. Divide feta cheese and olives
among the cakes. Serve at room
temperature.

THINK AHEAD
Make up to 2 days in advance. Store in layers on
paper towels in an airtight container at room
temperature. Crisp in 200°C (400°F) Gas 6 oven for 3
minutes. Top 45 minutes before serving.

BABY BAKED POTATOES WITH SOUR CREAM AND CAVIAR

MAKES 20

20 tiny new potatoes, pricked
1 tbsp olive oil
2 tsp salt
125ml (4floz) sour cream
100g (3½ oz) black lumpfish caviar

Preheat oven to 200°C (400°F) Gas 6.
Toss potatoes with oil and salt until
evenly coated. Place on a baking sheet
and cook until soft inside and crisp
outside, about 30 minutes. Cool
completely. Cut a cross on top of each
potato and squeeze gently to open.
Top each baby potato with 1 tsp each
sour cream and caviar. Serve at once.

THINK AHEAD
Bake potatoes up to 1 day in advance. Store in an
airtight container in the refrigerator. Crisp in a
preheated 200°C (400°F) Gas 6 oven for 5 minutes.
Top just before serving.

KIWI AND PASSIONFRUIT MINI PAVLOVAS

MAKES 20

1 recipe baked vanilla mini meringues (see page 141)

75ml (2½ floz) whipping cream

1 tbsp caster sugar

1 kiwi

2 passion fruit, halved

20 raspberries

2 tsp icing sugar for dusting

Whip cream until it holds soft peaks. Whisk in 1 tbsp caster sugar (see page 144). Cut kiwi in half and cut each half into 5 slices. Cut each slice in half. Scoop out pulp from passion fruit halves. Top each pavlova with 1 tsp cream. Arrange a half kiwi slice and a raspberry on top. Spoon over passion fruit and dust with icing sugar.

THINK AHEAD
Assemble meringues up to 3 hours in advance; keep at room temperature.

MUSCOVADO AND FIG MINI MERINGUES

MAKES 20

1 recipe baked muscovado mini meringues (see page 141)

2 figs

60g (2oz) plain chocolate, melted (see page 145)

125ml (4floz) crème fraîche

2 tsp cocoa powder for dusting

Cut figs in half, then slice each half into 5 slivers. Top individual meringues with 1 tsp crème fraîche and dust lightly with cocoa powder. Arrange 1 fig sliver on top then, using a teaspoon, drizzle with melted chocolate. Serve at room temperature.

THINK AHEAD
Assemble meringues up to 3 hours in advance; keep at room temperature.

STRAWBERRY AND PISTACHIO MINI MERINGUES

MAKES 20

1 recipe baked pistachio mini meringues (see page 141)

5 strawberries

75ml (2½ floz) whipping cream

1 tbsp caster sugar

2 tsp icing sugar for dusting

2 tbsp chopped pistachios

Cut strawberries into quarters. Whip cream until it holds soft peaks. Whisk in 1 tbsp caster sugar (see page 144). Top each meringue with 1 tsp cream and dust with icing sugar. Arrange strawberry quarters on top. Garnish with chopped pistachios.

THINK AHEAD
Assemble meringues 3 hours before serving; keep at room temperature.

HAZELNUT AND RASPBERRY MINI MERINGUES

MAKES 20

1 recipe baked hazlenut mini meringues (see page 141)

75ml (2½ floz) whipping cream

1 tbsp caster sugar

250g (8oz) raspberries

2 tsp icing sugar for dusting

20 tiny mint sprigs

Whip cream until it holds soft peaks. Whisk in 1 tbsp caster sugar (see page 144). Top each pavlova with 1 tsp cream. Arrange raspberries on top and dust with icing sugar. Garnish with mint sprigs.

THINK AHEAD
Assemble meringues up to 3 hours in advance; keep at room temperature.

POLENTA CROSTINI

MAKES 20

850ml (1pint 5floz) water
175g (6oz) instant polenta
1 tsp salt
4 tbsp grated parmesan cheese
½ tsp black pepper
2 tbsp olive oil

ESSENTIAL EQUIPMENT
500g (1lb) oiled loaf tin

Bring water to the boil in a large pan. Stir in the polenta and salt. Cook, stirring constantly, until thick, 5–10 minutes. Add parmesan and pepper. Pour hot polenta into the oiled tin (see below). Cool completely. Unmold polenta from the tin. Slice into 10 slices (see below). Cut each slice diagonally into 2 triangles. Place triangles onto oiled baking sheets. Brush triangles with oil. Place under a preheated grill until lightly golden and crisp, 3 minutes. Cool to room temperature before topping.

THINK AHEAD
Make polenta and leave in tin up to 3 days in advance. Cover and refrigerate. Cut and grill polenta up to 2 hours in advance. Keep at room temperature.

COOKS' NOTE
Add 2 crushed garlic cloves and 1 tbsp finely chopped herbs – rosemary, thyme or oregano – to the cooked, hot polenta for a little extra flavour.

Pour into an oiled loaf tin.

Unmold polenta from the tin and slice.

POLENTA CROSTINI WITH BLUE CHEESE AND BALSAMIC RED ONIONS

MAKES 20
2 tbsp olive oil
2 medium red onions, sliced
½ tsp salt
1 tbsp balsamic vinegar
black pepper
1 recipe polenta crostini (see opposite)
125g (4oz) dolcelatte or Danish blue cheese, crumbled

Heat oil in a pan over medium heat. Add onions and salt. Cook, stirring occasionally, until soft and tender, 10 minutes. Add vinegar and cook until evaporated, 3 minutes. Add pepper to taste. Cool to room temperature. Divide onions evenly among crostini, then top each one with 1 tsp crumbled cheese. Serve at room temperature.

THINK AHEAD
Cook onions up to 1 day in advance. Cover and store at room temperature. Top crostini 1 hour in advance. Keep at room temperature.

POLENTA CROSTINI WITH TOMATO AND BLACK OLIVE SALSA

MAKES 20
2 ripe tomatoes, peeled, seeded and diced (see page 147)
1 medium red onion, finely chopped
45g (1½oz) pitted black olives, finely chopped
2 tsp olive oil
1 tsp red wine vinegar
salt, pepper
1 recipe polenta crostini (see opposite)

Combine tomatoes, onion, olives, oil and vinegar. Add salt and pepper to taste. Cover and let stand at room temperature for 30 minutes to allow the flavours to blend.
Top polenta crostini with salsa. Serve at room temperature.

THINK AHEAD
Make salsa up to 1 day in advance but do not add salt and pepper until just before using. Store in an airtight container in the refrigerator. Top crostini 1 hour in advance. Keep at room temperature.

TOSTADITAS

MAKES 24

3 - 15cm (6in) flour tortillas
½ tbsp sunflower oil
¼ tsp salt

Preheat oven to 200°C (400°F) Gas 6.
Brush tortillas on one side with oil.
Cut each tortilla into 8 even-sized
wedges with kitchen scissors or a
serrated knife. Arrange oiled side up
in a single layer on an oiled baking
sheet. Sprinkle with salt. Bake until
crisp, 5–7 minutes. Cool on a wire
rack.

THINK AHEAD
Make tostaditas up to 5 days in advance. Store
in an airtight container at room temperature.

COOKS' NOTE
Good quality bought corn chips can be used as
a time-saving alternative. Be sure to buy plain,
lightly salted chips, not ones that are flavoured
with spices. A flavoured chip won't allow you to
appreciate the delicious topping.

TOSTADITAS WITH ROAST CORN SALSA

MAKES 24

½ corn on the cob
½ red pepper, seeded and quartered
½ green chilli, seeded and finely chopped
½ medium red onion, finely chopped
1 tbsp finely chopped coriander
1 tbsp lime juice
1 tbsp olive oil
salt, black pepper
1 recipe tostaditas (see opposite)

Preheat oven to 180°C (350°F) Gas 4.
Rinse corn under cold water to moisten. Place corn and pepper quarters on an oven
tray. Roast for 25 minutes. Remove pepper and peel (see page 147). Roast corn for a
further 20 minutes.
Cut the pepper into fine dice. When corn is cool, slice roasted kernels from the cob
with a sharp knife. Combine corn, peppers, chilli, onion, coriander, lime and oil. Add
salt and pepper to taste. Cover and refrigerate for 1 hour to allow flavours to blend.
Top tostaditas with salsa. Serve chilled or at room temperature.

THINK AHEAD
Make salsa up to 1 day in advance, but do not add the coriander more than 3 hours before serving. Cover
and refrigerate. Top tostaditas and serve immediately.

COOKS' NOTE
Oven roasting the corn is an important step as it allows the natural sugar in the corn to caramelize. It also
adds a nutty, smoky flavour to the corn's natural sweetness.

TOSTADITAS WITH CITRUS CEVICHE

MAKES 24

125g (4oz) halibut fillet
juice of 1 lime
juice of ½ lemon
2 tbsp orange juice
1 red chilli, seeded and finely chopped
1 spring onion, white stem only, finely chopped
1 tomato, seeded and diced (see page 147)
1 small avocado, diced
2 tbsp finely chopped coriander
½ tsp salt
1 recipe tostaditas (see page 59)

Cut the fish into fine dice. Combine fish with the lime, lemon and orange juices in a non-metallic bowl. Cover and refrigerate for 3 hours, stirring occasionally. Drain fish well, discarding all but 1 tbsp marinade. Toss the fish, chilli, spring onion, tomato, avocado, coriander, salt, and reserved 1 tbsp marinade together to combine. Top tostaditas with equal amounts of the ceviche. Serve chilled.

THINK AHEAD
Make ceviche up to 1 day in advance, but do not add the avocado, salt and coriander more than 3 hours before serving. Press cling film tightly over the surface of the ceviche and refrigerate. Top tostaditas just before serving.

COOKS' NOTE
Fresh tuna, salmon or scallops also make excellent ceviche. Use cooked prawns if you prefer not to use raw fish.

TOSTADITAS WITH BLACKENED SNAPPER, PEACH RELISH AND SOUR CREAM

MAKES 24

¼ tsp dried thyme
¼ tsp dried oregano
¼ tsp paprika
¼ tsp cumin seeds
¼ tsp garlic powder
½ tsp salt, ¼ tsp black pepper
125g (4oz) red snapper fillet, 1cm (½in) thick
2 tsp sunflower oil
1 stoned peach, fresh or tinned, finely diced
2 tsp lemon juice
1 recipe tostaditas (see page 59)
5 tbsp sour cream to garnish

Combine thyme, oregano, paprika, cumin, garlic, salt and pepper on a plate. Cut fish into 24 - 1cm (½in) cubes. Dip fish first in oil, then roll in spice mixture. Preheat a dry frying pan over a medium heat until very hot. Add fish cubes, spiced side down. Cook cubes 2 minutes per side until firm to the touch. Remove from pan and cool.
For relish, combine peach and lemon juice. Divide relish evenly among tostaditas. Top with fish. Garnish with sour cream. Serve chilled or at room temperature.

THINK AHEAD
Cook fish up to 1 day in advance. Cover and refrigerate. Make relish up to 1 day in advance. Cover and refrigerate. Top tostaditas up to 45 minutes before serving.

MINI POPPADOMS WITH CREAMY CHICKEN TIKKA

MAKES 30

30 mini poppadoms
1 tbsp sunflower oil
1 boneless, skinless chicken breast
2.5cm (1in) fresh ginger, grated
1 garlic clove, crushed
½ tsp ground cardamon
½ tsp ground cumin
½ tsp salt, ¼ tsp black pepper
1 tbsp lemon juice
4 tbsp Greek-style yoghurt
½ tsp paprika for sprinkling
30 coriander leaves to garnish

Preheat oven to 200°C (400°F) Gas 6. Place mini poppadoms in a single layer on an oiled baking sheet. Brush with oil. Bake until crisp and golden, 3–5 minutes. Cool on a wire rack.
Cut chicken into 0.5cm (¼in) thick slices. Combine chicken, ginger, garlic, spices, salt, pepper, lemon and yoghurt in a non-metallic bowl. Cover and refrigerate for at least 1 hour.
Place chicken under a preheated grill until cooked through, 8–10 minutes. Cool. Roughly chop.
Divide chicken evenly among the poppadoms. Sprinkle with paprika and garnish with coriander leaves. Serve chilled or at room temperature.

THINK AHEAD
Bake poppadoms up to 2 days in advance. Store in an airtight container at room temperature. Marinate chicken up to 1 day in advance. Cook chicken up to 1 day in advance. Cover and refrigerate. Top poppadoms up to 1 hour before serving.

COOKS' NOTE
Look for mini poppadoms at speciality food halls and Indian markets. If you have difficulty finding them, this Indian-inspired topping is also delicious served on tostaditas.

GINGERED CHICKEN CAKES WITH CORIANDER-LIME MAYONNAISE

MAKES 20

FOR CAKES

2 boneless, skinless chicken breasts

2 tbsp fish sauce

2.5cm (1in) fresh ginger, roughly chopped

3 spring onions, roughly chopped

1 garlic clove, crushed

1 tsp salt, ¼ tsp Tabasco

FOR TOPPING

4 tbsp mayonnaise (see page 142)

15g (½oz) coriander, finely chopped

juice of 1 lime

2 tbsp diced mango to garnish

20 coriander leaves to garnish

Preheat oven to 200°C (400°F) Gas 6. For cakes, place all cake ingredients in a food processor or blender; pulse until finely minced. Divide mixture into 20 walnut-sized pieces. With wet hands, shape each piece into a ball and flatten into a cake. Place cakes on an oiled baking sheet and cook until golden and cooked through, 12 minutes. Cool to warm or room temperature.

For topping, combine mayonnaise, coriander and lime. Spoon topping on to cakes. Garnish with mango and coriander leaves. Serve warm or at room temperature.

THINK AHEAD

Assemble cakes and prepare topping up to 1 day in advance. Cover and refrigerate. Bake and top cakes up to 1 hour in advance. Keep at room temperature. Garnish and serve.

COOKS' NOTE

Try using pork fillet instead of chicken and lemon grass instead of ginger for a tasty variation on these Asian-inspired minced cakes.

COCKTAIL SALMON AND DILL CAKES WITH CREME FRAICHE TARTARE

MAKES 20

FOR CAKES

150g (5oz) salmon fillet

200g (7oz) potatoes

2 tbsp roughly chopped dill

2 tbsp tomato ketchup

1 tsp horseradish sauce

1 tsp lemon juice

1 tsp salt, ¼ tsp Tabasco

2 tbsp fresh breadcrumbs

FOR TOPPING

4 tbsp crème fraîche

1 tsp drained capers, finely chopped

1 tsp drained cocktail gherkins, finely chopped

1 tsp finely chopped tarragon

salt, black pepper

20 watercress sprigs to garnish

Place salmon in pan of boiling water. Allow water to return to a boil, then remove pan from heat at once. Leave to cool completely. Drain on paper towels. Separate cooked salmon into large flakes.

Preheat oven to 200°C (400°F) Gas 6. Cook potatoes in boiling water until tender; mash until smooth. Combine potatoes with salmon, dill, ketchup, horseradish sauce and lemon. Add salt and Tabasco to taste. Divide mixture into 20 walnut-sized pieces. Shape pieces into balls and roll in breadcrumbs. Flatten into cakes and place on an oiled baking sheet. Bake until golden, 10 minutes. Cool to warm or room temperature.

For topping, combine all topping ingredients. Add salt and pepper to taste. Spoon topping on to cakes. Garnish with watercress. Serve warm or at room temperature.

THINK AHEAD

Assemble cakes and prepare topping up to 1 day in advance. Cover and refrigerate. Bake and top cakes up to 1 hour in advance. Keep at room temperature. Garnish just before serving.

MINI DEVILLED CRAB CAKES WITH TOMATO REMOULADE

MAKES 20

FOR CAKES

250g (8oz) white crab meat
½ onion, finely chopped
½ tsp runny honey
½ tsp mustard powder
½ tsp Tabasco
1 tsp Worcestershire sauce
1 tsp horseradish sauce
1 tsp lemon juice
3 tbsp mayonnaise (see page 142)
7–9 tbsp fresh breadcrumbs
salt, black pepper

FOR TOPPING

4 tbsp mayonnaise (see page 142)
2 tsp finely chopped chives
1 tsp lemon juice
½ tsp creamy Dijon mustard
½ tsp garlic, finely chopped
salt, black pepper
1 tomato, peeled, seeded, chopped and diced (see page 147)
finely chopped chives to garnish

For cakes, mix crab, onion, honey, mustard powder, Tabasco, Worcestershire and horseradish sauces, lemon and mayonnaise together. Add enough fresh breadcrumbs to bind, about 2–4 tbsp. Add salt and pepper to taste. Divide mixture into heaped teaspoonfuls, about 20 walnut-sized pieces. Shape each piece into a ball and roll lightly in remaining crumbs. Place on an oiled baking sheet. Refrigerate until firm, 30 minutes. Preheat oven to 200°C (400°F) Gas 6. Bake crab cakes until crisp and golden, 10 minutes. Cool to warm or room temperature.
For topping, combine mayonnaise, chives, lemon, mustard and garlic. Add salt and pepper to taste. Spoon topping on to crab cakes. Garnish with tomato and chives. Serve warm or at room temperature.

THINK AHEAD
Assemble cakes and make topping up to 1 day in advance. Cover and refrigerate. Bake and top cakes up to 1 hour before serving.

AUBERGINE AND PINE NUT FRITTERS WITH ROAST TOMATO SAUCE

MAKES 20

FOR TOPPING

2 plum tomatoes, halved
1 garlic clove, sliced
1 tsp balsamic vinegar
½ tsp runny honey
½ tsp finely chopped rosemary
salt, black pepper

FOR FRITTERS

2 tbsp olive oil
1 medium aubergine, diced
1 garlic clove, crushed
1 tbsp finely chopped parsley
1 tsp finely chopped rosemary
1 egg plus 1 egg yolk, beaten
75g (2½oz) parmesan cheese, grated
100g (3½oz) mozzarella cheese, diced
60g (2oz) dry breadcrumbs
60g (2oz) pine nuts, roughly chopped
salt, black pepper
20 small rocket leaves to garnish

Preheat oven to 200°C (400°F) Gas 6.
For topping, put tomatoes and garlic on oven tray. Drizzle with vinegar and honey and sprinkle with rosemary, salt and pepper. Roast in oven until softened, 20 minutes. Cool and place in a food processor or blender; pulse until smooth. For fritters, heat oil in a skillet over medium-high heat. Stir-fry diced aubergine until soft and golden, 10 minutes. Drain and cool on kitchen paper. Combine with garlic, parsley, rosemary, beaten eggs, parmesan, mozzarella, breadcrumbs and pine nuts. Add salt and pepper to taste. Divide mixture into 20 walnut-sized pieces. Shape each piece into an oval. Place ovals on an oiled baking sheet. Bake until golden, 10 minutes. Cool to warm or room temperature. Spoon topping on to cakes. Garnish with rocket. Serve warm or at room temperature.

THINK AHEAD
Assemble fritters and prepare topping up to 1 day in advance. Cover and refrigerate. Cook and top fritters up to 1 hour in advance. Keep at room temperature. Garnish just before serving.

MINI STICKY ORANGE AND ALMOND CAKES

MAKES 25

2 whole oranges, unpeeled
6 eggs, beaten
250g (8oz) granulated sugar
250g (8oz) ground almonds
1 tsp baking powder
4 tbsp pomegranate kernels
to garnish (see below)
150ml (5floz) Greek-style yoghurt

ESSENTIAL EQUIPMENT

35 x 25cm (14 x 10in) Swiss roll tray lined with buttered baking parchment, 4.25cm (¾ in) pastry cutter

Cook whole oranges in boiling water until soft, 1½ hours. Cool completely. Preheat oven to 190°C (375°F) Gas 5. For cake, cut oranges in half and remove any pips. Place in a food processor; process to a smooth purée. Add eggs, sugar, almonds and baking powder; pulse until well combined. Pour batter into the lined tray. Bake until firm to the touch, 40 minutes. Cool completely. Cut pomegranate in half through the middle of the stem end. Cut each half into quarters (see below, top right). Pull stem ends of each quarter towards each other, bending peel back to release pomegranate kernels (see below, bottom right). Stamp cake into 20 rounds with the pastry cutter (see below, left). Spoon ½ tsp yoghurt on to each cake round. Garnish with pomegranate kernels. Serve at room temperature.

THINK AHEAD

Make cake up to 2 days in advance. Store at room temperature. Alternatively, bake and freeze cake up to 1 month in advance (see page 149). Defrost in the refrigerator overnight. Garnish cakes up to 3 hours ahead. Leave at room temperature, until ready to serve.

MINI CHOCOLATE TRUFFLE CAKES

MAKES 25

FOR CAKE

150g (5oz) butter
400g (14oz) dark chocolate, broken into pieces
150g (5oz) granulated sugar
5 eggs, separated
45g (1½oz) flour

FOR GLAZE

5 tbsp double cream
75g (2½oz) dark chocolate, broken into pieces

ESSENTIAL EQUIPMENT

35 - 25cm (14 x 10in) Swiss roll tray lined with buttered baking parchment, 4.25cm (1¾in) pastry cutter

Preheat oven to 150°C (300°F) Gas 2.
For cake, melt butter and chocolate together in a double boiler over low heat. Stir continuously until smooth and melted. Remove from heat and cool to tepid. Beat sugar, egg yolks and flour into the cool chocolate. Whisk egg whites until they hold soft peaks (see page 141). Gently fold chocolate mixture into whites until evenly combined. Pour batter into the lined tray. Bake until firm to the touch, 20 minutes. Cool completely.
For glaze, heat cream in a pan just below the boiling point. Remove from heat. Stir in chocolate until melted and smooth. Cool until slightly thickened, 30 minutes. Stamp cooled cake into 25 rounds with the pastry cutter. Spoon 1 heaped teaspoonful glaze over each cake round. Serve at room temperature.

THINK AHEAD

Bake cake up to 5 days in advance. Store at room temperature. Alternatively, bake and freeze cake up to 1 month in advance (see page 149). Defrost in refrigerator overnight. Cut and glaze cake rounds up to 3 hours in advance. Leave at room temperature, until ready to serve.

Cut pomegranate into quarters.

Stamp out cake rounds.

Pull back peel to release kernels.

STICKS AND SKEWERS

PROSCIUTTO-WRAPPED SCALLOP BROCHETTES WITH SAUCE BEARNAISE

MAKES 20

20 queen scallops or 10 sea scallops
7 very thin prosciutto slices
20 large basil leaves
salt, black pepper
1 recipe sauce bearnaise (see page 143)

ESSENTIAL EQUIPMENT
20 - 15cm (6in) wooden skewers presoaked in cold water

If using sea scallops, slice in half crosswise. Cut each prosciutto slice into 3 strips. Place 1 basil leaf on top of each prosciutto strip. Place 1 queen scallop or ½ sea scallop on top. Sprinkle with a pinch of both salt and pepper. Wrap basil and prosciutto around each scallop. Secure each wrapped scallop with 1 presoaked skewer.
Preheat grill. Alternatively, preheat a ridged cast-iron griddle, grill pan or barbecue. Grill or griddle scallop brochettes until scallops have turned from opaque to white, 1–2 minutes on each side. Serve hot, warm or at room temperature with sauce bearnaise.

THINK AHEAD
Skewer scallops up to 8 hours in advance. Store in an airtight container in the refrigerator.

TANGY THAI PRAWN SKEWERS

MAKES 20

20 tiger prawns, cooked and peeled
2 garlic cloves, finely chopped
1cm (½in) piece fresh ginger, grated
1 red chilli, seeded and finely chopped
1 tsp granulated sugar
1 tbsp fish sauce
juice of 1 lime

ESSENTIAL EQUIPMENT
20 - 7.5cm (3in) wooden skewers or toothpicks

Pat prawns dry with paper towels. Combine prawns, garlic, ginger, chilli, sugar, sauce and lime in a non-metallic bowl. Cover and refrigerate for 1 hour. Skewer 1 prawn on to each skewer. Serve chilled.

THINK AHEAD
Marinate prawns up to 6 hours in advance. Skewer prawns up to 3 hours in advance. Store in an airtight container in the refrigerator.

COOKS' NOTE ON GRILLING WITH SKEWERS

Don't forget to presoak wooden skewers when using them in a grilled recipe. Allow the skewers to soak for at least 30 minutes in cold water to prevent them from scorching.

BARBECUED TANDOORI PRAWN STICKS

MAKES 20

125ml (4floz) Greek-style yoghurt
2 tbsp lemon juice
3 garlic cloves, crushed
2.5cm (1in) piece fresh ginger, grated
1 tsp turmeric
1 tsp paprika
¼ tsp ground cardamom
¼ tsp cayenne pepper, 1 tsp salt
20 raw tiger prawns, peeled and deveined (see page 164)

ESSENTIAL EQUIPMENT
20 - 7.5cm (3in) wooden skewers or toothpicks presoaked in cold water

For marinade, combine yoghurt, lemon, garlic, ginger, spices and salt in a non-metallic bowl. Add prawns and toss in marinade to coat each one well. Cover and refrigerate for 1 hour. Thread 1 prawn on to each presoaked skewer. Preheat grill. Alternatively, preheat a ridged cast-iron griddle, grill pan or barbecue. Grill prawns until they turn pink and lose their transparency, 3 minutes on each side. Serve hot, warm or at room temperature.

THINK AHEAD
Marinate prawns up to 4 hours in advance. Store in an airtight container in the refrigerator. Skewer prawns up to 1 hour in advance. Store in an airtight container in the refrigerator.

GRAPEFRUIT SCALLOP CEVICHE SKEWERS

MAKES 20

40 queen scallops or 20 sea scallops
grated zest and juice of 1 grapefruit
juice of 2 limes
4 tbsp olive oil
1 fresh red chilli, seeded and finely
chopped
½ red onion, finely chopped
½ tsp salt
1 tbsp finely chopped coriander
1 spring onion, finely sliced

ESSENTIAL EQUIPMENT
20 - 7.5cm (3in) wooden skewers or toothpicks

If using sea scallops, slice in half
crosswise. Combine scallops, grapefruit,
lime, oil, chilli, onion and salt in a
non-metallic bowl. Cover and refrigerate
for 3 hours, stirring occasionally.
Remove scallops with a slotted spoon.
Toss to coat with coriander and spring
onion. Thread 2 queen scallops or 2 sea
scallop halves on to each skewer.
Serve chilled.

THINK AHEAD
Marinate scallops up to 6 hours in advance. Skewer
scallops up to 3 hours in advance. Store in an
airtight container in the refrigerator.

COOKS' NOTE
If you are uncomfortable about serving raw fish, use
cooked, peeled tiger prawns instead of raw scallops.

LEMON CHILLI PRAWN STICKS

MAKES 20

2 garlic cloves, crushed
1cm (½in) piece fresh ginger, grated
2 tbsp finely chopped coriander
½ tbsp Chinese hot chilli sauce
1 tbsp light soy sauce
1 tbsp runny honey
3 tbsp lemon juice
20 raw tiger prawns, peeled and deveined (see page 164)

ESSENTIAL EQUIPMENT
20 - 15cm (6in) wooden skewers presoaked in cold water

For marinade, combine garlic, ginger, coriander, chilli sauce, soy sauce, honey and
lemon in a non-metallic bowl. Add prawns and toss in marinade to coat each one
well. Cover and refrigerate for 1 hour. Thread 1 prawn on to each presoaked
skewer. Preheat grill. Alternatively, preheat a ridged cast-iron griddle, grill pan or
barbecue. Grill prawns until they turn pink and lose their transparency, 3 minutes
on each side. Serve hot, warm or at room temperature.

THINK AHEAD
Marinate prawns up to 4 hours in advance. Store in an airtight container in the refrigerator. Skewer prawns
up to 1 hour in advance. Store in an airtight container in the refrigerator.

PRAWN AND SUGARCANE STICKS WITH MINTED CHILLI DIPPING SAUCE

MAKES 20

4 - 10cm (4in) long sugarcane pieces
500g (1lb) raw prawns, peeled and
deveined (see page 164)
2 garlic cloves, chopped
3 spring onions, chopped
1 tbsp fish sauce
1 tsp sugar
1 tbsp cornflour
1 egg white

1 tsp salt
½ tsp black pepper

FOR SAUCE

1 tbsp finely chopped mint
1 fresh green chilli, seeded
and finely chopped
1 tbsp sugar
6 tbsp lime juice
6 tbsp fish sauce

Peel sugarcane with a vegetable peeler. Cut each sugarcane
piece into 0.5cm (¼in) thick strips to make 20 sugarcane
sticks (see page 148). Place prawns, garlic, spring onions, fish
sauce, sugar, cornflour, egg white, salt and pepper in a food
processor or blender; pulse to a smooth paste. Divide prawn
paste into 20 equal-sized pieces. With wet hands, place
1 piece of prawn paste in the middle of your palm. Place
sugarcane stick in the middle of the paste. Mould prawn paste
around the end of the stick. Repeat with remaining paste and
sticks. Cover prawn sticks and refrigerate for 30 minutes.
For sauce, combine mint, chilli, sugar, lime and fish sauce.
Let stand at room temperature for 15 minutes to allow the
flavours to blend.
Preheat grill or barbecue. Grill prawn sticks until golden and
cooked through, 3 minutes on each side. Serve warm.

THINK AHEAD
Mould prawn paste on to sugarcane sticks up to 4 hours in advance. Store in
an airtight container in the refrigerator. Make dipping sauce without mint up to
3 days in advance. Cover and refrigerate. Add mint up to 3 hours before
serving. Keep covered at room temperature.

COOKS' NOTE
You can find fresh, frozen or tinned sugarcane from Asian food stores. Wooden
skewers are less exotic, but can be used for this fragrant prawn paste.

MANGETOUT-WRAPPED PRAWN SKEWERS WITH LEMON MAYONNAISE

MAKES 20

20 large mangetout
20 large prawns, cooked and peeled
1 recipe lemon mayonnaise (see page 142)

ESSENTIAL EQUIPMENT
20 - 15cm (6in) wooden skewers

Bring a pan of water to a boil over hight heat. Add mangetout
and boil for 1 minute. Drain and refresh mangetout in cold
water. Drain again and pat dry with paper towels.
Place 1 prawn on top of each mangetout. Secure with skewer.
Cover and refrigerate for 30 minutes. Serve chilled with lemon
mayonnaise.

THINK AHEAD
Skewer prawns and mangetout up to 8 hours in advance. Store in an airtight
container in the refrigerator.

SALMON TERIYAKI SKEWERS WITH GINGER SOY DIPPING SAUCE

MAKES 20

350g salmon fillet, 2.5cm (1in) thick

FOR GLAZE

3 tbsp sake

3 tbsp mirin

5 tbsp shoyu (Japanese soy sauce)

1½ tbsp caster sugar

FOR SAUCE

1cm (½in) piece fresh ginger, finely chopped

2 spring onions, finely sliced

juice of 2 limes

6 tbsp shoyu (Japanese soy sauce)

ESSENTIAL EQUIPMENT

20 - 15cm (6in) wooden skewers or chopsticks presoaked in cold water

Cut salmon into 20 - 2.5cm (1in) cubes.

For glaze, place sake, mirin, soy and sugar in a small pan. Bring to a boil over medium heat. Simmer gently for 10 minutes until thick and syrupy. Cool.

For sauce, whisk ginger, spring onions, lime and soy together. Let stand at room temperature for 15 minutes to allow the flavours to blend.

Toss salmon with cooled glaze in a non-metallic bowl to coat each piece well. Leave to marinate at room temperature for 10 minutes. Thread 1 salmon cube on to 2 skewers or chopsticks.

Preheat grill. Alternatively, preheat a ridged cast-iron griddle, grill pan or barbecue. Grill salmon skewers until firm to the touch, 2–3 minutes on each side. Serve hot or warm with ginger soy dipping sauce.

THINK AHEAD

Skewer salmon up to 3 hours in advance. Store in an airtight container in the refrigerator. Make dipping sauce without spring onions up to 3 days in advance. Cover and refrigerate. Add spring onions up to 3 hours before serving. Keep covered at room temperature.

MONKFISH, PANCETTA AND ROSEMARY SPIEDINI WITH LEMON AIOLI

MAKES 20

350g (12oz) monkfish tail, boned and skinned

4 pancetta or bacon slices

20 - 10cm (4in) rosemary branches

FOR MARINADE

4 tbsp olive oil

grated zest and juice of ½ lemon

1 garlic clove, sliced

1 tsp salt, ½ tsp black pepper

1 recipe lemon aioli (see page 142)

Cut the monkfish into 20 - 2.5cm (1in) cubes. Cut pancetta into 20 equal-sized pieces. Cover pancetta and refrigerate.

For rosemary skewers, pull the leaves off the rosemary stalks, leaving just a few leaves at one end. Reserve leaves. Sharpen the other end into a point with a sharp paring knife (see page 148).

For marinade, roughly chop the reserved rosemary leaves. Combine rosemary, oil, lemon, garlic, salt and pepper in a non-metallic bowl. Add monkfish and toss to coat each piece well. Cover and refrigerate for 30 minutes.

Thread 1 monkfish cube and 1 bacon piece on to the pointed end of each rosemary skewer. Preheat grill. Alternatively, preheat a ridged cast-iron griddle, grill pan or barbecue. Grill monkfish spiedini until cooked through, 2–3 minutes on each side. Serve warm with lemon aioli.

THINK AHEAD

Marinate monkfish up to 4 hours in advance. Store in an airtight container in the refrigerator. Skewer up to 2 hours in advance. Store in an airtight container in the refrigerator.

COOKS' NOTE

If you are using an overhead grill to cook the spiedini, make sure that the rosemary-sprigged end protrudes from the oven so as not to catch fire.

MOROCCAN SPICED SWORDFISH BROCHETTES

MAKES 20

350g (12oz) swordfish steak, 2.5cm (1in) thick

FOR MARINADE

1 red pepper, quartered and seeded
1 red chilli, seeded and chopped
2 garlic cloves, chopped
2 tbsp chopped coriander
2 tbsp chopped parsley
½ tsp ground coriander
1 tsp runny honey
grated zest and juice of ½ lemon
2 tbsp olive oil
1 tsp salt, ¼ tsp black pepper

ESSENTIAL EQUIPMENT

20 - 15cm (6in) wooden skewers presoaked in cold water

Cut swordfish into 20 - 2.5cm (1in) cubes. For marinade, grill and peel pepper quarters (see page 147). Place peeled pepper quarters, chilli, garlic, fresh herbs, ground coriander, honey, lemon, oil and salt and pepper in a food processor or blender; pulse to a thick paste. Toss swordfish and marinade together in a non-metallic bowl to coat each piece well. Cover and refrigerate for at least 30 minutes.
Thread 1 swordfish cube on to each presoaked skewer.
Preheat grill. Alternatively, preheat a ridged cast-iron griddle, grill pan or barbecue. Grill swordfish brochettes until cooked through, 2–3 minutes on each side. Serve hot or warm.

THINK AHEAD

Marinate swordfish up to 4 hours in advance. Store in an airtight container in the refrigerator. Skewer up to 2 hours in advance. Store in an airtight container in the refrigerator.

CHAR-GRILLED MEDITERRANEAN TUNA SKEWERS WITH SPICY ROAST TOMATO DIP

MAKES 20

350g (12oz) tuna steak, 2.5cm (1in) thick

FOR MARINADE

15g (½oz) basil
15g (½oz) parsley
2 garlic cloves
grated zest and juice of ½ lemon
2 tbsp olive oil
1 tsp salt
½ tsp black pepper
20 large basil leaves

ESSENTIAL EQUIPMENT

20 - 15cm (6in) wooden skewers presoaked in cold water

FOR DIP

6 plum tomatoes, halved
1 red chilli, seeded and chopped
2 garlic cloves, chopped
1 tbsp olive oil
1 tbsp balsamic vinegar
salt, black pepper

For marinade, place basil, parsley, garlic, lemon, oil, salt and pepper in a food processor or blender; pulse to a thick paste. Toss tuna and marinade together in a non-metallic bowl to coat each piece well. Cover and refrigerate for at least 30 minutes.
For dip, preheat oven to 200°C (400°F) Gas 6. Place tomatoes on an oven tray. Sprinkle over chilli, garlic, oil, vinegar and a pinch each salt and pepper. Roast until softened, 30 minutes. Place in a food processor or blender; pulse until smooth. Push through a sieve to remove seeds. Add salt and pepper to taste. Keep warm.
Cut tuna into 2.5cm (1in) cubes. Wrap each tuna cube in a basil leaf. Thread 1 wrapped tuna cube on to each presoaked skewer. Preheat grill. Alternatively, preheat a ridged cast-iron griddle, grill pan or barbecue. Grill tuna skewers until cooked through, 2–3 minutes on each side. Serve hot or warm with spicy roast tomato dip.

THINK AHEAD

Make dip up to 2 days in advance. Cover and refrigerate. Marinate tuna up to 4 hours in advance. Store in an airtight container in the refrigerator. Skewer up to 2 hours in advance. Store in an airtight container in the refrigerator. Reheat dip just before serving.

COOKS' NOTE

Oven roasting tomatoes concentrates their flavour and is a very good treatment for out of season or less than ripe tomatoes.

CURRIED COCONUT CHICKEN STICKS

MAKES 20

2 boneless, skinless chicken breasts

FOR MARINADE

4 lemon grass stalks

1 tbsp curry powder

4 garlic cloves, chopped

5cm (2in) piece fresh ginger, chopped

2 shallots, chopped

15g (½ oz) coriander

4 tbsp fish sauce

125ml (4floz) tinned coconut milk

1 tsp salt, ¼ tsp black pepper

ESSENTIAL EQUIPMENT

20 - 15cm (6in) wooden skewers presoaked in cold water

Cut chicken into 20 - 2.5cm (1in) cubes.

For marinade, remove and discard the tough outer skin from the lemon grass stalks and finely chop. Place lemon grass, curry powder, garlic, ginger, shallots, coriander, fish sauce, coconut milk, salt and pepper in a food processor or blender; pulse until smooth. Toss chicken and marinade together in a non-metallic bowl to coat each piece well. Cover and refrigerate for at least 1 hour.

Thread 1 chicken cube on to each presoaked skewer. Preheat grill. Alternatively, preheat a ridged cast-iron griddle, grill pan or barbecue. Grill chicken sticks until cooked through, 5 minutes on each side. Serve hot, warm or at room temperature.

THINK AHEAD

Marinate chicken up to 1 day in advance. Skewer chicken up to 12 hours in advance. Store in an airtight container in the refrigerator.

LEMON AND SAFFRON CHICKEN BROCHETTES

MAKES 20

2 boneless, skinless chicken breasts

FOR MARINADE

1 large pinch of saffron

½ medium onion, finely chopped

grated zest and juice of 1 lemon

4 tbsp olive oil

1 tsp salt, ½ tsp black pepper

ESSENTIAL EQUIPMENT

20 - 15cm (6in) wooden skewers presoaked in cold water

Cut chicken into 20 - 2.5cm (1in) cubes. For marinade, combine saffron, onion, lemon, oil, salt and pepper in a non-metallic bowl. Add chicken and toss to coat each piece well. Cover and refrigerate for at least 1 hour.

Thread 1 chicken cube on to each presoaked skewer. Preheat grill. Alternatively, preheat a ridged cast-iron griddle, grill pan or barbecue. Grill chicken brochettes until cooked through, 5 minutes on each side.

Serve hot or warm.

THINK AHEAD

Marinate chicken up to 1 day in advance. Skewer chicken up to 12 hours in advance. Store in an airtight container in the refrigerator.

COOK'S NOTE

An important reminder: don't forget to presoak wooden skewers when using them in a grilled recipe. Allow the skewers to soak for at least 30 minutes in cold water to prevent them from scorching.

CHICKEN, PROSCIUTTO AND SAGE SPIEDINI WITH ROAST PEPPER AIOLI

MAKES 20

FOR AIOLI

1 red pepper, quartered and seeded
1 recipe lemon aioli (see page 142)

FOR SPIEDINI

2 boneless, skinless chicken breasts
2 tbsp lemon juice
1 garlic clove, crushed

1 tsp salt
½ tsp black pepper
4 tbsp olive oil
5 prosciutto slices
20 sage leaves
4 slices day-old baguette, 2.5cm (1in) thick

ESSENTIAL EQUIPMENT
20 -15cm (6in) wooden skewers presoaked in cold water

For aioli, grill and peel pepper quarters (see page 147). Place peeled pepper quarters in a food processor or blender; pulse to a smooth purée. Stir pepper purée into aioli. Let stand at room temperature for 15 minutes to allow the flavours to combine.
For spiedini, cut chicken into 2.5cm (1in) cubes. Toss chicken together with lemon, garlic, salt, pepper and 4 tbsp oil in a non-metallic bowl to coat each piece well.
Cut each prosciutto slice into 4 strips. Place 1 sage leaf on each prosciutto strip. Top with 1 chicken cube. Wrap sage and prosciutto around chicken. Repeat with remaining chicken.
Cut baguette slices into 20 - 2.5cm (1in) cubes. Thread 1 bread cube and 1 prosciutto-wrapped chicken cube on to each presoaked skewer. Brush bread with remaining oil.
Preheat grill. Alternatively, preheat a ridged cast-iron griddle, grill pan or barbecue. Grill chicken spiedini until cooked through, 5 minutes on each side. Serve warm or at room temperature with roast pepper aioli.

THINK AHEAD
Make aioli up to 3 days in advance. Cover and refrigerate. Skewer chicken up to 12 hours in advance. Store in an airtight container in the refrigerator.

THAI CHICKEN AND LEMON GRASS STICKS WITH SWEET CUCUMBER DIPPING SAUCE

MAKES 20

11 lemon grass stalks
2 boneless, skinless chicken breasts
2 garlic cloves, chopped
1 red chilli, seeded and chopped
2 tbsp chopped coriander
1 tsp brown sugar
1 tsp salt

FOR SAUCE

125ml (4floz) rice vinegar
125g (4oz) granulated sugar
2 garlic cloves, finely chopped
2 red chillies, seeded and finely chopped
½ tsp salt
¼ cucumber, seeded and finely diced
1 tbsp finely chopped coriander

For lemon grass sticks, remove and discard the tough outer skin from the lemongrass. Set 1 stalk aside to flavour the chicken. Cut each of the 10 remaining lemon grass stalks in half lengthwise, keeping the stalks attached by the root. Trim to 12.5cm (5in) lengths (see page 148).
Place the reserved lemon grass stalk, chicken, garlic, chilli, coriander, sugar and salt in a food processor; pulse to a smooth paste. Divide into 20 equal-sized pieces. With wet hands, roll into oval shapes. Skewer each chicken oval on to the slimmer end of each lemon grass length. Cover and refrigerate for 30 minutes to allow the flavours to blend.
For sauce, bring vinegar and sugar to a boil in a pan over medium heat. Simmer gently until syrupy, 5 minutes. Pour syrup over garlic, chillies and salt. in a separate bowl and cool. Stir in cucumber and coriander when cool. Let stand for 15 minutes at room temperature to allow the flavours to combine. Preheat grill. Alternatively, preheat a ridged cast-iron griddle, grill pan or barbecue. Grill chicken lemon grass sticks until cooked through, 5 minutes on each side. Serve hot, warm or at room temperature with sweet cucumber dipping sauce.

THINK AHEAD
Prepare and skewer chicken up to 12 hours in advance. Store in an airtight container in the refrigerator. Make sauce without cucumber and coriander up to 3 days in advance. Cover and refrigerate. Add cucumber and coriander up to 3 hours before serving. Keep covered at room temperature.

CHICKEN YAKITORI

MAKES 20

350g (12oz) boneless, skinless chicken thighs

FOR MARINADE

4 tbsp shoyu (Japanese soy sauce)

2 tbsp mirin

1½ tbsp sake

1 tsp caster sugar

5 shiitake mushrooms

2 spring onions

ESSENTIAL EQUIPMENT

20 - 15cm (6in) wooden skewers presoaked in cold water

Cut chicken into 20 - 2.5cm (1in) pieces. For marinade, place soy, mirin, sake and sugar in a small pan. Bring to a boil over a medium heat. Simmer gently until slightly syrupy, 5 minutes. Cool. Toss marinade and chicken together in a non-metallic bowl to coat each piece well. Cover and refrigerate for at least 30 minutes.
Cut mushrooms into quarters. Cut spring onions in 20 - 2.5cm (1in) lengths. Thread 1 spring onion piece, 1 chicken cube and 1 mushroom quarter on to each presoaked skewer. Preheat grill. Alternatively, preheat a ridged cast-iron griddle, grill pan or barbecue. Grill chicken yakitori until cooked through, 5 minutes on each side. Serve hot.

THINK AHEAD
Marinate chicken up to 3 hours in advance. Assemble skewers up to 1 hour in advance. Store in an airtight container in the refrigerator.

LIME MARINATED CHICKEN SKEWERS WITH AVOCADO CREMA DIP

MAKES 20

2 boneless, skinless chicken breasts

FOR MARINADE

juice of 1 lime

1 tbsp runny honey

2 tbsp olive oil

2 green chillies, deseeded and finely chopped

15g (½oz) coriander, finely chopped

1tsp salt, ¼ tsp black pepper

ESSENTIAL EQUIPMENT

20 - 15cm (6in) wooden skewers presoaked in cold water

FOR DIP

1 avocado, stoned

3 spring onions, chopped

1 tbsp red wine vinegar

1 tbsp olive oil

125ml (4floz) sour cream

salt, black pepper

1 tbsp finely chopped coriander to garnish

Cut chicken into 2.5cm (1in) cubes.
For marinade, combine lime, honey, oil, chillies, coriander, salt and pepper in a non-metallic bowl. Add chicken and toss to coat each piece well. Cover and refrigerate for at least 1 hour.
For dip, place avocado, spring onions, vinegar, olive oil and sour cream in a food processor or blender; pulse until smooth. Add salt and pepper to taste. Cover and refrigerate for 30 minutes to allow the flavours to blend.
Thread a chicken cube on to each presoaked skewer. Preheat grill. Alternatively, preheat a ridged cast-iron griddle, grill pan or barbecue. Grill chicken skewers until cooked through, 5 minutes on each side. Garnish each skewer with a sprinkling of coriander. Serve warm with avocado crema dip.

THINK AHEAD
Marinate chicken up to 1 day in advance. Skewer chicken up to 12 hours in advance. Store in an airtight container in the refrigerator. Make dip up to 8 hours in advance. Cover and refrigerate.

COOKS' NOTE
To prevent the avocado crema dip from discolouring when making ahead, make sure you press a piece of cling film directly on to the surface of the dip. It's the oxygen in the air that turns avocado brown, so the less air that comes into contact with the dip, the better.

SPICY SATAY STICKS

MAKES 20

2 boneless, skinless chicken breasts

FOR MARINADE
1 lemon grass stalk
2 shallots
2 garlic cloves
1cm (½in) piece fresh ginger
2 tsp brown sugar
½ tsp ground cumin
½ tsp ground coriander
1 tsp turmeric
1 tsp salt
1 tbsp sunflower oil

ESSENTIAL EQUIPMENT
20 - 15cm (6in) wooden skewers presoaked in cold water

FOR SAUCE
4 tbsp roasted peanuts
2 lemon grass stalks
2 shallots
2 garlic cloves
2.5cm (1in) piece fresh ginger
1 tsp turmeric
1 tbsp sunflower oil
1 tbsp brown sugar
1 tsp fish sauce
1 tbsp Chinese hot chilli sauce
juice of 1 lime
4 tbsp water
125ml (4floz) coconut milk

Slice chicken into 20 strips about 0.5cm (¼in) thick and 6cm (2½in) long.

For marinade, remove and discard the tough outer skin from the lemon grass and finely chop. Place lemon grass, shallots, garlic, ginger, sugar, spices, salt and oil in a food processor or blender; pulse to a smooth paste. Toss chicken and marinade together in a non-metallic bowl to coat each piece well. Cover and refrigerate for at least 1 hour.

For sauce, place peanuts in a food processor or blender; pulse until finely ground. Set aside. Remove and discard the tough outer skin from the lemon grass and finely chop. Place shallots, garlic, ginger, chopped lemon grass, turmeric and sunflower oil in a food processor or blender; pulse to a smooth paste. Heat a frying pan over a medium heat. Add paste and stir fry until softened, 5 minutes. Stir in ground peanuts, sugar, fish sauce and chilli sauce, lime, water and coconut milk. Cook, stirring occasionally, until the sauce thickens, 10 minutes. Keep warm.

Thread 1 chicken strip on to each presoaked skewer, running the skewer through it like a ruffled ribbon. Preheat grill. Alternatively, preheat a ridged cast-iron griddle, grill pan or barbecue. Grill chicken satay sticks until cooked through, 5 minutes on each side. Serve hot with warm satay sauce.

THINK AHEAD
Make sauce up 4 days in advance. Cover and refrigerate. Marinate chicken up to 1 day in advance. Skewer chicken up to 12 hours in advance. Store in an airtight container in the refrigerator. Reheat sauce before serving.

COOKS' NOTE
The satay sauce will thicken on standing, so, if making ahead, bear in mind that you may need to thin it down with a tablespoon or so of lime juice when you reheat.

CUMIN SCENTED KOFTE BROCHETTES WITH MINTED YOGHURT DIP

MAKES 20

350g (12oz) lean minced lamb

1 medium onion, grated

2 garlic cloves, chopped

2 tsp ground cumin

½ tsp ground coriander

grated zest of 1 lemon

2 tbsp finely chopped coriander

1½ tsp salt

¼ tsp cayenne pepper

FOR DIP

175ml (6floz) Greek-style yoghurt

15g (½oz) mint, finely chopped

15g (½oz) parsley, finely chopped

juice of ½ lemon

salt, cayenne pepper

ESSENTIAL EQUIPMENT

20 - 15cm (6in) wooden skewers presoaked in cold water

Place lamb, onion, garlic, cumin, ground coriander, lemon, fresh coriander, salt and cayenne pepper in a food processor; pulse until combined and slighly pasty. Divide into 20 equal-sized pieces. With wet hands, roll into oval shapes. Thread 1 oval on to each presoaked skewer. Cover and refrigerate for 30 minutes. For dip, combine yoghurt, mint, parsley and lemon. Add salt and cayenne pepper to taste. Cover and refrigerate for 30 minutes to allow the flavours to blend. Preheat grill. Alternatively, preheat a ridged cast-iron griddle, grill pan or barbecue. Grill brochettes until browned but still pink and juicy inside, 3 minutes on each side. Serve hot with chilled minted yoghurt dip.

THINK AHEAD

Make dip up to 1 day in advance. Cover and refrigerate. Prepare and skewer kofte up to 12 hours in advance. Store in an airtight container in the refrigerator.

SESAME SOY GLAZED BEEF SKEWERS

MAKES 20

350g (12oz) beef fillet or sirloin, 2.5cm (1in) thick

4 spring onions, white stalk only

1 red pepper, halved and seeded

FOR GLAZE

2 tbsp sesame seeds

2 lemon grass stalks, tender stalk only, finely chopped

1 tbsp runny honey

2 tbsp sesame oil

1 tbsp sunflower oil

2 tbsp light soy sauce

1 tbsp Chinese hot chilli sauce

½ tsp black pepper

1 tsp salt

ESSENTIAL EQUIPMENT

20 - 15cm (6in) wooden skewers presoaked in cold water

Cut beef into 20 - 2.5cm (1in) cubes. Cut spring onions diagonally into 20 - 2.5cm (1in) lengths. Cut pepper into 20 - 2.5cm (1in) pieces.

For glaze, combine seeds, lemon grass, honey, oils, soy sauce, chilli sauce, black pepper and salt in a non-metallic bowl. Add beef, spring onions, and peppers. Toss to coat each piece well. Cover and refrigerate for at least 1 hour.

Thread 1 piece each of spring onion and pepper and 1 beef cube on to each presoaked skewer.

Preheat grill. Alternatively, preheat ridged cast-iron griddle, grill pan or barbecue. Grill beef skewers until browned but still pink and juicy inside, 3 minutes on each side. Serve hot.

THINK AHEAD

Marinate beef up to 1 day in advance. Store in an airtight container in the refrigerator. Skewer beef up to 12 hours in advance. Store in an airtight container in the refrigerator.

MINT MARINATED LAMB KEBABS WITH TAHINI AND HONEY DIP

MAKES 20

350g (12oz) lean boneless lamb

FOR MARINADE

30g (1oz) mint, finely chopped
2 garlic cloves, crushed
1 tbsp runny honey
2 tbsp lemon juice
2 tbsp olive oil
1 tsp salt
½ tsp pepper

FOR DIP

2 tbsp sesame seeds
2 tsp runny honey
juice of 1 lemon
5 tbsp tahini
125ml (4floz) Greek-style yoghurt
3 tbsp water
salt, black pepper

ESSENTIAL EQUIPMENT
20 - 15cm (6in) wooden skewers presoaked in cold water

Cut lamb into 20 - 2.5cm (1in) cubes.
For marinade, combine half of the chopped mint, garlic, honey, lemon juice, oil, salt and pepper. Add lamb and toss to coat each piece well. Cover and refrigerate. Leave to marinate for at least 1 hour.
For dip, toast seeds in a dry pan over low heat until nutty and golden, 3 minutes. Combine seeds, honey, lemon, tahini, yoghurt and water. Add salt and pepper to taste. Cover and refrigerate. Leave for 30 minutes for the flavours to blend.
Thread 1 lamb cube on to each presoaked skewer. Preheat grill. Alternatively, preheat ridged cast-iron griddle, grill pan or barbecue. Grill lamb kebabs until browned but still pink and juicy inside, 3 minutes on each side. Garnish each kebab with a sprinkling of the remaining mint. Serve hot with chilled tahini and honey dip.

THINK AHEAD
Make dip up to 2 days in advance. Cover and refrigerate. Marinate lamb up to 1 day in advance. Skewer lamb up to 12 hours in advance. Store in an airtight container in the refrigerator.

GINGER ORANGE PORK SKEWERS

MAKES 20

350g (12oz) lean boneless pork

FOR MARINADE

5cm (2in) piece fresh ginger, grated
grated zest of 1 orange
juice of ½ orange
2 tsp creamy Dijon mustard
2 tsp runny honey

1 tbsp balsamic vinegar
2 tbsp light soy sauce
4 tbsp olive oil
1 tsp salt
½ tsp black pepper
5cm (2in) piece fresh ginger for garnish

ESSENTIAL EQUIPMENT
20 - 15cm (6in) wooden skewers presoaked in cold water

Cut pork into 20 - 2.5cm (1in) cubes. Combine grated ginger, orange, mustard, honey, vinegar, soy, oil, salt and pepper in a non-metallic bowl. Add pork and toss to coat each piece well. Cover and refrigerate for at least 1 hour.
For garnish, preheat oven to 200°C (400°F) Gas 6. Cut ginger piece for garnish into fine slices. Cut ginger slices into julienne (see page 147). Bring a pan of water to a boil over high heat. Add ginger julienne and boil for 1 minute. Drain. Spread ginger julienne in a single layer on a baking sheet. Bake until crispy and dry, 5–10 minutes. Cool.
Preheat grill. Alternatively, preheat ridged cast-iron griddle, grill pan or barbecue. Grill pork skewers until cooked through, 5 minutes on each side. Sprinkle each skewer with crisp ginger garnish. Serve hot.

THINK AHEAD
Make crisp ginger garnish up to 2 days in advance. Store in an airtight container at room temperature. Marinate pork up to 1 day in advance. Store in an airtight container in the refrigerator. Skewer pork up to 12 hours in advance. Store in an airtight container in the refrigerator.

TROPICAL FRUIT BROCHETTES WITH PASSION FRUIT AND MASCARPONE DIP

MAKES 20

1 firm mango

2 firm kiwi

¼ watermelon

FOR DIP

2 passion fruit, halved

200g (7oz) mascarpone cheese

1 tbsp runny honey

1 tbsp grated orange zest

ESSENTIAL EQUIPMENT

20 wooden toothpicks

Cut each fruit into 20 - 2cm (¾in) cubes. Thread 3 different fruit cubes on to each skewer. Cover and refrigerate for 30 minutes.

For dip, spoon passion fruit pulp out from the centre of each half with a teaspoon. Sieve pulp and discard seeds. Combine passion fruit pulp, mascarpone, honey and orange. Cover and refrigerate for 30 minutes. Serve chilled tropical fruit brochettes with chilled passion fruit and mascarpone dip.

THINK AHEAD

Make dip up to 1 day in advance. Cover and refrigerate. Skewer fruit up to 4 hours in advance. Cover and refrigerate.

COOKS' NOTE

These brochettes are open to variation. Use your favourite combination of tropical fruit. For the prettiest brochettes, think about complementary colours as well as flavours. Try to select firm, just ripe fruits that will cube and skewer easily.

PROSCIUTTO-WRAPPED FIG SKEWERS

MAKES 20

10 very thin prosciutto slices

100g (3½oz) parmesan cheese

5 ripe figs, quartered

black pepper

½ tbsp grated parmesan cheese

ESSENTIAL EQUIPMENT

vegetable peeler

20 - 15cm (6in) wooden skewers

Cut each prosciutto slice lengthways into 2 strips. Shave the parmesan with a vegetable peeler to make 20 shavings (see page 148). Place 1 parmesan shaving on each prosciutto strip. Place 1 fig quarter on top. Sprinkle with a pinch of pepper. Wrap up the fig in prosciutto. Secure with skewer. Sprinkle with grated parmesan just before serving. Serve chilled or at room temperature.

THINK AHEAD

Wrap and skewer figs up to 4 hours in advance. Cover and refrigerate.

COOKS' NOTE

Firm melon and papaya slices make suitable substitutes when figs are not in season. Speck, coppa or serrano are a few of the huge wealth of cured hams that are suitable alternatives to prosciutto. To make wrapping easy, make sure any ham you choose is sliced very thin.

CHERUBS ON HORSEBACK

MAKES 20

20 ready-soaked dried apricots

10 slices of unsmoked streaky bacon

ESSENTIAL EQUIPMENT

20 wooden toothpicks presoaked in cold water

Preheat oven 200°C (400°F) Gas 6. Cut the bacon in half widthways. Stretch each piece of bacon by running the back of a knife along the bacon slice. This will help prevent shrinking during cooking. Wrap 1 bacon piece around each apricot. Secure with a presoaked skewer. Place skewered apricots on an oven tray. Bake until bacon is crisp, 10 minutes. Serve hot or warm.

THINK AHEAD

Wrap and skewer apricots up to 1 day in advance. Store in an airtight container in the refrigerator.

LEMON MARINATED TORTELLINI AND SUN-DRIED TOMATO SKEWERS

MAKES 20
20 fresh spinach and ricotta tortellini
10 sun-dried tomatoes in oil,
drained and halved
20 large basil leaves

FOR MARINADE
1 tsp grated lemon zest
2 tbsp lemon juice
4 tbsp olive oil
salt, black pepper

ESSENTIAL EQUIPMENT
20 - 15cm (6in) wooden skewers

Cook tortellini in salted boiling water
until tender, 4 minutes, or according to
instructions on the packet. Drain and
rinse with cold water. Spread out in a
single layer on a clean tea towel to dry.
For marinade, whisk lemon and oil until
thick and combined. Toss the cooled
pasta and marinade together in a
non-metallic bowl to coat each piece
well. Add salt and pepper to taste.
Cover and marinate at room
temperature for 30 minutes. Thread
1 tortellini and 1 sun-dried tomato half
wrapped in 1 basil leaf on to each
skewer. Serve at room temperature.

THINK AHEAD
Marinate tortellini up to 1 day in advance. Cover and
refrigerate. Assemble skewers up to 4 hours in
advance. Return to room temperature before serving.

BASIL MARINATED MOZZARELLA AND CHERRY TOMATO SKEWERS

MAKES 20
1 red pepper, quartered and seeded
1 garlic clove, finely chopped
1 tbsp lemon juice
2 tbsp olive oil
½ tsp salt
1 tsp cracked black pepper
20 bocconcini (baby mozzarella balls)
15g (½oz) basil, finely chopped
20 cherry tomatoes, halved
20 large basil leaves

ESSENTIAL EQUIPMENT
20 - 15cm (6in) wooden skewers

Grill and peel pepper quarters (see
page 147). Cut pepper quarters into
very fine dice (see page 147). Combine
pepper dice, garlic, lemon, oil, salt and
cracked pepper in a non-metallic bowl.
Add bocconcini and toss to coat each
piece well. Cover and marinate at room
temperature for at least 30 minutes.
Sprinkle basil over and toss to coat each
bocconcini well. Thread 1 cherry tomato
half and 1 bocconcini on to each skewer.
Wrap each remaining cherry tomato half
in 1 basil leaf and add 1 to each skewer.
Serve chilled or at room temperature.

THINK AHEAD
Marinate bocconcini up to 3 days in advance. Store
in an airtight container in the refrigerator. Assemble
skewers up to 4 hours in advance. Cover and
refrigerate.

COOKS' NOTE
Bocconcini means "mouthful" in Italian. If you can't
find these baby mozzarella balls, cut whole mozzarella
cheese (you'll need 1 large one) into 20 - 2cm (¾ in)
cubes, then marinate and skewer as directed.

FENNEL MARINATED FETA AND OLIVE SKEWERS

MAKES 20
2 tbsp sesame seeds
200g (7oz) feta cheese
1 tbsp fennel seeds
grated zest of 1 lemon
1 tbsp lemon juice
2 tbsp olive oil
1½ tsp cracked black pepper
15g (½oz) mint, finely chopped
½ cucumber, peeled and seeded
20 mint leaves
10 pitted black olives, halved

ESSENTIAL EQUIPMENT
20 - 5cm (6in) wooden skewers

Toast seeds in a dry pan over low heat
until nutty and golden, 3 minutes. Cool.
Gently rinse feta in cold water. Drain on
kitchen paper. Cut feta into 2cm (¾in)
cubes. Toss feta together with fennel,
toasted sesame seeds, lemon, oil and
pepper to coat each cube well. Cover
and refrigerate for 4 hours to allow the
flavours to combine.
Sprinkle feta with chopped mint and
toss to coat each cube well. Cut
cucumber into 20 - 1cm (½in) cubes.
Thread 1 mint leaf, 1 olive half,
1 cucumber cube and 1 feta cube on to
each skewer. Serve chilled or at room
temperature.

THINK AHEAD
Marinate feta up to 3 days in advance. Store in an
airtight container in the refrigerator. Skewer feta up
to 4 hours in advance. Cover and refrigerate.

WRAPS AND ROLLS

SPINACH, SMOKED TROUT AND HERBED CREAM ROULADE

MAKES 30

FOR ROULADE

350g (12oz) spinach

3 eggs, separated

1 tsp salt

½ tsp black pepper

¼ tsp ground nutmeg

FOR FILLING

200g (7oz) cream cheese

2 tbsp finely chopped fresh dill

grated zest and juice of 1 lemon

salt, black pepper

200g (7oz) smoked salmon slices

ESSENTIAL EQUIPMENT

35 x 25cm (14 x 10in) Swiss roll tray lined with buttered baking parchment

Preheat oven to 200°C (400°F) Gas 6. Bring a pan of water to a boil and add spinach. When the water returns to a boil, drain and refresh the spinach in cold water. Squeeze spinach dry with hands. Place spinach, egg yolks, salt, pepper and nutmeg in a food processor or blender; pulse to a smooth purée. Whisk egg whites until they hold soft peaks (see page 141). Fold egg whites lightly into the spinach until evenly combined. Spread spinach mixture into the prepared tray. Bake until set, 10–12 minutes. Turn baked roulade out on to a sheet of baking parchment. Leave to cool. For filling, combine cream cheese, dill, lemon zest and juice. Add salt and pepper to taste. Peel off tray lining paper. Cut roulade in half widthways. Place each half on a piece of cling film. Spread filling evenly over both roulade halves, to within about 1 cm (½ in) of the edges. Cover each with a layer of salmon slices. Sprinkle with black pepper. Roll up each roulade half from the long edge. Wrap in cling film, twisting the ends to secure (see page 148). Refrigerate rolls 1 hour. With a serrated knife, trim ends of both roulades. Cut each roulade into 10 slices. Discard cling film after slicing. Serve chilled or at room temperature.

THINK AHEAD

Make roulade up to 1 day in advance. Refrigerate. Slice up to 1 hour before serving.

ROLLED PARSLEY FRITTATINE WITH BLACK OLIVE RICOTTA

MAKES 20

FOR FRITTATINE

3 eggs, beaten

3 tbsp double cream

1 tbsp melted butter

1 tbsp finely chopped parsley

⅛ tsp ground nutmeg

½ tsp salt, ¼ tsp pepper

1 tsp butter for pan

FOR FILLING

125g (4oz) ricotta cheese

150g (5oz) pitted black olives, finely chopped

salt, black pepper

ESSENTIAL EQUIPMENT

24cm (9in) non-stick or heavy frying pan

Beat eggs, cream, melted butter, parsley, nutmeg, salt and pepper until combined. Melt half of the butter in pan over medium heat. Pour in half of egg mixture. Cook until golden and set on both sides, 5 minutes in total. Slide frittatine from pan on to kitchen paper to drain. Repeat with remaining butter and egg mixture. Leave to cool. For filling, combine ricotta and olives. Add salt and pepper to taste. Spread each cooled frittatina evenly with half of the filling to within 1cm (½in) of edges. Roll up separately. Wrap each in cling film, twisting the ends to secure (see page 148). Refrigerate 1 hour. With a serrated knife, trim ends of both frittatina. Cut each frittatina into 10 slices. Discard the cling film after slicing. Serve chilled or at room temperature.

THINK AHEAD

Make frittatine up to 1 day in advance. Refrigerate. Slice up to 1 hour before serving.

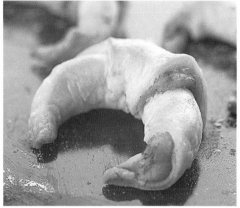

HAM AND DIJON MINI CROISSANTS

MAKES 20

250g (8oz) puff pastry
3 tbsp creamy Dijon mustard
125g (4oz) ham slices
1 egg yolk beaten with 1 tbsp water

Preheat oven to 200°C (400°F) Gas 6. Roll out pastry to 45cm x 18cm (18in x 7in) rectangle. Trim uneven edges with a sharp knife. Cut pastry in half lengthwise to make 2 strips each 9cm (3½in) wide. Cut each strip diagonally into 10 even-sized triangles (see below, left). Cut ham into strips about 10cm (4in) long and 0.5cm (¼in) wide. Spread each pastry triangle with mustard. Place ham on longest edge. Roll up each triangle, starting at the long edge and ending with the point (see below, right). Place on an oiled baking sheet. Curl ends in to make a crescent. Tuck the points underneath to prevent the croissants from unravelling as they bake. Brush croissants with beaten egg. Bake until crisp and golden, 10 minutes. Cool on wire rack. Serve warm or at room temperature.

THINK AHEAD
Bake up to 3 days in advance. Store in an airtight container at room temperature. Crisp in preheated 200°C (400°F) Gas 6 oven, 3 minutes.

Mark out the triangle shapes with the back of a knife before cutting.

SMOKED SALMON RUGGELASH

MAKES 32

FOR PASTRY
90g (3oz) cream cheese
90g (3oz) cold butter, diced
125g (4oz) plain flour
pinch salt

FOR FILLING
200g (7oz) smoked salmon slices
1 tbsp lemon juice
¼ tsp black pepper
1 tbsp finely chopped fresh dill
1 egg yolk beaten with 1 tbsp water

Preheat oven to 200°C (400°F) Gas 6. Place cream cheese, butter, flour and salt in a food processor; pulse until smooth dough forms. Refrigerate 30 minutes. Divide pastry into 2 equal-sized pieces. Roll out each piece to a 23cm (9in) round. Cover each round with a single layer of smoked salmon slices. Cut each round across into 16 even-sized triangles. Sprinkle with lemon, pepper and dill. Roll up each triangle, starting at the long edge and ending with the point. Place on an oiled baking sheet. Curl ends in to make a crescent. Tuck the points underneath to prevent the ruggelash from unravelling as they bake. Refrigerate until firm, 20 minutes. Brush ruggelash with beaten egg. Bake until crisp and golden, 10 minutes. Cool on wire rack. Serve warm.

THINK AHEAD
Bake up to 3 days in advance. Store in an airtight container at room temperature. Crisp in preheated 200°C (400°F) Gas 6 oven, 3 minutes.

QUEEN OLIVE CHEESE BALLS

MAKES 20

20 pitted large green olives
75g (2½oz) parmesan cheese, grated
60g (2oz) cold butter, diced
100g (3½oz) plain flour
salt, cayenne pepper
1 egg yolk beaten with 1 tbsp water
1 tsp poppy seeds

Preheat oven 180°C (350°F) Gas 4. Pat olives dry with kitchen paper. Place parmesan, butter and flour with pinch each salt and cayenne pepper in a food processor; pulse until smooth pastry forms. Divide pastry into 20 equal-sized pieces. With floured hands, press 1 piece of pastry around each olive to enclose completely. Roll pastry-wrapped olives between palms of your hands to make smooth, olive shapes. Place on an oiled baking sheet. Refrigerate until firm, 30 minutes. Brush pastry with beaten egg. Sprinkle with seeds. Bake until golden, 20 minutes. Cool on a wire rack. Serve warm or at room temperature.

THINK AHEAD
Bake up to 3 days in advance. Store in an airtight container at room temperature. Crisp in preheated 200°C (400°F) Gas 6 oven, 3 minutes.

COOKS' NOTE
If you can't find pitted large green olives, use 30 regular pitted olives instead.

SPICY PORK EMPANADITAS WITH CHUNKY AVOCADO RELISH

MAKES 20

FOR FILLING

1 tbsp sunflower oil
½ medium onion, finely chopped
175g (6oz) minced pork
3 garlic cloves, finely chopped
1 red chilli, seeded and
finely chopped
½ tsp ground cumin
¼ tsp ground cinnamon
pinch of ground cloves
125ml (4floz) tomato juice
1 tsp tomato purée
2 tbsp raisins
10 pimento-stuffed green olives,
chopped
salt, black pepper

FOR PASTRY

175g (6oz) flour
½ tsp salt
30g (1oz) butter
90ml warm water

ESSENTIAL EQUIPMENT

1 - 6.5 (2¾ in) plain pastry cutter

FOR RELISH

½ medium onion, finely
chopped
2 red chillies, seeded and
finely chopped
2 tomatoes, peeled, seeded
and finely chopped
(see page 147)
1 garlic clove, finely
chopped
2 tbsp finely chopped
coriander
juice of 1 lime
2 medium avocados
salt

For filling, heat oil in a frying pan over medium heat.
Stir-fry onions in oil until soft, 5 minutes. Add pork. Stir pork
constantly with a fork to break up any lumps, until lightly
browned, 5 minutes. Add garlic and chilli and cook until
fragrant, 3 minutes. Add spices, tomato juice, tomato purée,
raisins and olives. Reduce heat to low and simmer, stirring
occasionally, until thick, 15 minutes. Cool. Add salt and
pepper to taste. Cover and refrigerate until chilled, 30 minutes.
For pastry, sift flour and salt into a bowl. Rub butter into the
flour with fingers until mixture resembles fine crumbs. Use a
fork to stir in the water to make a firm dough. Turn dough on
to a lightly floured surface and knead until smooth, 3 minutes.
Wrap dough in cling film and let rest at room temperature for
30 minutes. Roll out dough to a 2mm (⅛in) thickness. Stamp
out 20 rounds with the pastry cutter. Place 1 tsp of filling in
centre of each round. Fold pastry over filling to make
crescents. Pinch edges firmly together to seal. With fingertips,
crimp edges (see opposite).
Place empanaditas on oiled baking sheets. Brush with
beaten egg. Bake until crisp and golden, 15 minutes. Cool on
a wire rack.
For relish, combine onion, chilli, tomato, garlic, coriander and
lime. Cut avocados into 2.5cm (1in) cubes. Mash the avocado
into the onion mixture while combining with the other
ingredients. Add salt to taste. Cover cling film tightly over the
surface of the relish. Refrigerate for 15 minutes.
Serve empanaditas warm or at room temperature with relish
for dipping.

EMPANADITAS FILLING VARIATIONS

SPICY CHORIZO EMPANADITAS

Use 175g (6oz) skinned and crumbled chorizo sausage instead
of minced pork when making the filling.

HOT PEPPER AND SMOKY MOZZARELLA EMPANADITAS

Make hot pepper relish (see page 119). Fill the pastry rounds
with 1 tsp grated smoked mozzarella and 1 tsp relish instead of
spicy pork mixture.

THINK AHEAD

Assemble empanaditas up to 1 day in advance. Cover and refrigerate. Bake
empanaditas up to 8 hours in advance. Keep at room temperature. Make relish
up to 3 hours in advance. Cover tightly with cling film and refrigerate.

COOKS' NOTE

The secret to juicy empanaditas is to chill the filling before assembling. The juices
in the filling will solidify so that the empanaditas won't leak as they are assembled.
Press a piece of cling film directly on to the surface of the relish to keep out the
air that causes the avocado to darken. If the relish does discolour slightly, simply
scrape off the dark surface. The relish will still be green underneath.

CRAB AND PAPAYA RICE PAPER ROLLS WITH SWEET CHILLI DIPPING SAUCE

MAKES 20

125g (4oz) white crab meat
2 spring onions, cut into julienne strips
(see page 147)
½ cucumber, seeded and cut into
julienne strips (see page 147)
10 sheets of rice paper
1 papaya, quartered and finely sliced
20 mint leaves
20 basil leaves

FOR SAUCE

2 tbsp sugar
2 tbsp boiling water
2 tbsp fish sauce
2 tbsp lime juice
1 tbsp rice vinegar
1 red chilli, seeded and
chopped
1 garlic, crushed

Divide the crab, spring onions and cucumber strips into 20 equal-sized portions.
Pour about 1.5cm (¾in) cold water into a shallow dish. Dip 1 sheet of rice paper into the water and leave to soften, 2 minutes. Remove and spread out on a dry tea towel. Cut in half. Top 1 half with 1 portion of crab, spring onion and cucumber. Place 1 papaya slice, 1 mint leaf and 1 basil leaf on top of the cucumber so that they stick out slightly over the straight end of the rice paper. Roll rice paper over to enclose filling. Fold one end of the rice paper over the enclosed filling to make a 5cm (2in) cylinder. Continue rolling up into a cylinder and press the end with a wet finger to seal. Place the roll, seal side down on a tray and cover with a dampened tea towel to keep moist. Repeat with the remaining half sheet rice paper, then start again with remaining rice paper sheets and filling.
For sauce, dissolve sugar in boiling water. Combine dissolved sugar, fish sauce, lime, vinegar, chilli and garlic.
Serve rice paper rolls chilled or at room temperature with sweet chilli dipping sauce.

THINK AHEAD
Prepare filling ingredients up to 1 day in advance. Cover and refrigerate. Make rolls up to 3 hours in advance. Cover with a dampened tea towel and refrigerate. Be sure to keep the tea towel moist.

COOKS' NOTE
Rice paper is fragile and fiddly to work with. Be prepared to discard some rice papers if they tear and have extra rice papers in reserve to replace them.

Enclose prawn in rice paper.

FRESH HERB AND PRAWN RICE PAPER ROLLS WITH PEANUT HOISIN DIPPING SAUCE

MAKES 20

1 carrot, cut into julienne strips
(see page 147)
1 tsp sugar
10 tiger prawns, cooked and peeled
5 small lettuce leaves
15g (½oz) coriander, separated into leaves
10 sheets of rice paper
20 mint leaves

FOR SAUCE

2 tbsp hoisin sauce
2 tbsp smooth peanut butter
1 tbsp tomato ketchup
5 tbsp water

Combine carrot strips with sugar and toss to coat each piece well. Let stand until wilted, 15 minutes.
Cut prawns in half lengthwise. Cut lettuce leaves into 5cm x 2.5cm (2in x 1in) strips. Divide carrots and coriander into 20 equal-sized portions. Set aside.
Pour about 1.5cm (¾in) cold water into a shallow dish. Dip 1 sheet of rice paper into the water and leave to soften, 2 minutes. Remove and spread out on a dry tea towel. Cut in half. Top 1 half sheet with 1 lettuce strip, 1 mint leaf and 1 portion each of carrots and coriander. Roll rice paper over to enclose filling. Fold both ends of rice paper over the enclosed filling. Place 1 prawn half, cut side down, on top (see below, left). Continue rolling up into a cylinder and press the end with a wet finger to seal. Place the roll, seal side down, on a tray and cover with a dampened tea towel to keep moist. Repeat with the remaining half sheet rice paper, then start again with remaining rice paper sheets and filling. For sauce, combine hoisin, peanut butter, ketchup and water. Serve rice paper rolls chilled or at room temperature with peanut hoisin dipping sauce.

THINK AHEAD
Prepare filling ingredients up to 1 day in advance. Cover and refrigerate. Make rolls up to 3 hours in advance. Cover with a dampened tea towel and refrigerate. Be sure to keep the tea towel moist.

SUSHI RICE

MAKES 300g (10oz)
175g (6oz) short-grained rice
200g (7floz) water
125ml (4floz) rice vinegar
5 tbsp sugar

Put rice in a large bowl. Cover with cold tap water and stir with your fingers until water turns cloudy. Pour off water. Repeat this 1 or 2 more times until water is almost clear. Drain rice in a sieve. Put drained rice in a pan, add 200g (7floz) water, cover, and bring to a boil over a high heat. Boil for 2 minutes. Reduce heat to low and simmer until water is absorbed and rice is tender, 15 minutes. Remove from heat and let stand without lifting the lid, for 5 minutes.

In separate pan, bring vinegar and sugar to boil over medium heat, stirring until the sugar dissolves. Remove from heat and cool. Turn the hot cooked rice out on to an oven tray and immediately drizzle the vinegar and sugar mixture evenly over the rice. Toss gently but thoroughly with a wooden spoon. Quickly cool the rice to room temperature by fanning it while continuing to toss the rice. Cover the rice with a dampened tea towel and cool completely.

THINK AHEAD
Make rice up to 3 hours in advance. Store covered with a dampened tea towel at room temperature.

COOKS' NOTE
Fanning the rice as it cools will make the rice especially glossy. Use a piece of stiff cardboard or a baking sheet if you don't have a fan.

CUCUMBER NORI SUSHI ROLLS

MAKES 24
2 tsp sesame seeds
2 sheets of nori, halved
1 recipe sushi rice (see opposite)
½ tsp wasabi paste
½ cucumber, seeded and cut into julienne strips (see page 147)
2 tbsp pickled ginger
6 tbsp shoyu (Japanese soy sauce)

ESSENTIAL EQUIPMENT
bamboo sushi mat

Toast seeds in a dry pan over low heat until nutty and golden, 3 minutes. Cool. Have a small bowl of water ready for moistening your fingers. Place 1 half piece nori, smooth side down, on the mat. Moisten your fingers with water, then spread a quarter of the rice in an even layer on the nori, leaving a 1cm (½in) strip uncovered at the end furthest away from you. Press down the rice with moistened fingers to pack firmly. Spread a thin line of wasabi lengthwise along the centre of the rice with your finger. Arrange a quarter of the cucumber, sesame seeds and ginger on top, making sure the fillings extend completely to each end of the rice. Pick up the bamboo mat and tightly roll rice around the filling, pulling the mat as you roll (see opposite). Unroll mat. Repeat with remaining nori, rice, wasabi, cucumber, sesame seeds and ginger. Cut each nori roll into 6 equal-sized pieces with a moist knife. Serve chilled or at room temperature with soy sauce for dipping.

THINK AHEAD
Make but do not cut nori rolls up to 1 day in advance. Store wrapped in cling film at room temperature.

SMOKED SALMON SUSHI RICE BALLS

MAKES 20
100g (3½oz) smoked salmon slices
1 recipe sushi rice (see opposite)
1 tsp wasabi paste

Cut salmon into 20 - 2.5cm (1in) squares. Divide the rice into 20 equal-sized portions. Cut cling film into 20 - 10cm (4in) squares. Place 1 piece of salmon in the centre of 1 cling film square. Place 1 portion of rice on top. Gather cling film around the rice and twist the ends to make a tight ball (see below, right). Repeat with remaining salmon, cling film and rice. Unwrap rice balls. Garnish with a knife's tip of wasabi. Serve chilled or at room temperature.

THINK AHEAD
Make rice balls up to 2 days in advance. Refrigerate wrapped. Garnish up to 1 hour before serving.

SUSHI RICE BALL VARIATIONS

SALMON CAVIAR SUSHI RICE BALLS

Omit smoked salmon. Replace wasabi garnish with 100g (3½oz) salmon caviar. Wrap rice in cling film as directed to make rice balls. Garnish each rice ball with 1 tsp salmon caviar up to 1 hour before serving.

TIGER PRAWN SUSHI RICE BALLS

Substitute smoked salmon with 10 cooked, peeled tiger prawns cut in half lengthwise. Place 1 prawn half cut side up on each piece of cling film. Top with rice and wrap in cling film as directed to make rice balls. Garnish with wasabi as directed.

THINK AHEAD
Make rice balls up to 2 days in advance. Refrigerate wrapped. Garnish up to 1 hour before serving.

Pull mat as you roll.   Twist to make tight balls.

MINI CALIFORNIA ROLLS

MAKES 40

5 sheets of nori
1 recipe sushi rice (see page 89)
½ cucumber, seeded and cut into julienne strips (see page 147)
1 avocado, finely sliced into 40 pieces
40 pickled ginger slices
1 tsp wasabi

ESSENTIAL EQUIPMENT
bamboo sushi mat

Fold nori sheets into three, lengthwise, to make a strip. Fold the strip into 3. Unfold and tear along the folded lines to make squares. Place the squares smooth side down. Have a small bowl of water ready for moistening your fingers. Place 1 half, smooth side down, on the mat. Divide the rice and cucumber into 40 equal-sized portions. Moisten your fingers with water, then spread 1 rice portion in an even layer over the left half of 1 nori square. Spread a thin line of wasabi lengthwise along the centre of the rice with your finger. Arrange 1 portion cucumber, 1 avocado slice and 1 ginger piece on top. Starting at the left corner, roll up the nori square like a cone, moistening with a wet finger to stick the nori together (see below, left).
Repeat with remaining nori, rice, wasabi, cucumber, avocado and ginger. Serve at room temperature.

THINK AHEAD
Assemble up to 1 hour in advance. Cover with cling film and store at room temperature.

SESAME SUSHI ROLLS

MAKES 24

3 tbsp sesame seeds
125g (4oz) medium prawns
2 sheets of nori, halved
1 recipe sushi rice (see page 89)
½ tsp wasabi paste

½ cucumber, seeded and cut into julienne strips (see page 147)
6 tbsp shoyu (Japanese soy sauce)

ESSENTIAL EQUIPMENT
bamboo sushi mat

Toast seeds in a dry pan over low heat until nutty and golden, 3 minutes. Cool. Cut prawns in half lengthwise.
Have a small bowl of water ready for moistening your fingers. Cut 1 sheet of cling film just larger than 1 nori half. Place 1 nori half, smooth side down, on the mat. Moisten your fingers with water, then spread a quarter of the rice in an even layer on the nori. Cover with the cling film. Pick up the nori, carefully turn over and place on the mat cling film side down. The nori should now be facing up. Spread a thin line of wasabi lengthwise along the centre of the nori with your finger. Arrange a quarter of the prawns, cucumber and 1tsp sesame seeds on top, making sure the fillings extend completely to each end. Pick up the bamboo mat and cling film and tightly roll rice around the filling, pressing down firmly as you roll. Unroll mat and cling film. Gently roll the rice roll in half the remaining sesame seeds (see opposite, centre). Roll up tightly in cling film, twisting the ends to secure (see opposite, right). Repeat with remaining nori, rice, wasabi, prawns, cucumber, and sesame seeds. Trim the ends of each roll to neaten, then cut each rice roll into 6 equal-sized pieces with a moist knife. Remove cling film from the cut pieces. Serve at room temperature with shoyu for dipping.

THINK AHEAD
Assemble but do not cut rice rolls up to 1 day in advance. Store wrapped in cling film at room temperature. Cut when ready to serve.

COOKS' NOTE
We used a mixture of black and brown sesame seeds for coating the roll that is pictured here. To make black sesame seeds, toast the seeds in a dry pan over a medium heat until blackened. For an alternative coating, try 2 tbsp red lumpfish roe.

WONTON WRAPPERS

MAKES 20

150g (5oz) plain flour
125ml (4floz) boiling water

ESSENTIAL EQUIPMENT
5cm (2in) plain pastry cutter

Place the flour in a bowl and make a well in the centre. Pour in the water. Mix with a fork to form a rough dough. Cover with a tea towel and let stand until cool enough to handle. Knead on a lightly floured surface until smooth and elastic, 5 minutes. Cover with a tea towel and let rest for 30 minutes. Roll out dough on a lightly floured surface to a 0.25cm (⅛in) thickness. Stamp out 20 rounds with the pastry cutter.

THINK AHEAD
Make up to 1 day in advance. Store in an airtight container stacked in single layers separated by greaseproof paper. Alternatively, freeze wrappers up to 1 month in advance. Store in a sealed plastic freezer bag stacked in single layers separated by cling film (see page 149). Defrost overnight in the refrigerator.

CRISPY WONTON CRESCENTS WITH GINGERED PORK AND CHILLI SOY DIPPING SAUCE

MAKES 20

75g (2½oz) lean minced pork
1 garlic clove, crushed
1 spring onion, chopped
2cm (¾in) piece ginger, grated
1 tbsp dark soy sauce
1 tsp sesame oil
1 recipe wonton wrappers, or 20 ready made round dumpling wrappers
2 tbsp plain flour for dusting
2 tbsp sunflower oil
250ml (8floz) cold water for cooking

FOR SAUCE
1 tbsp Chinese hot chilli sauce
4 tbsp dark soy sauce

ESSENTIAL EQUIPMENT
wok with a lid

CRISPY WONTON CRESCENT VARIATION

CRISPY WONTON CRESCENTS WITH HERBED PRAWN AND TANGY LIME DIPPING SAUCE

Place pork, garlic, spring onion, ginger, soy sauce and sesame oil in a food processor or blender; pulse until well combined. Place ½ tsp pork filling in the centre of each wrapper. Fold wrapper over to enclose filling to make crescents. Press edges together to seal. With fingertips, crimp edges (see page 86). Dip the bottom of each wonton crescent in a little flour. Place on a floured oven tray and cover with a damp tea towel. For sauce, combine chilli sauce and soy sauce.
Heat 1 tbsp oil in the wok over medium heat. When oil is very hot, add half the wonton crescents flat-side down to the wok in a single layer. Cook until crispy underneath, 5 minutes. Add to the centre of the wok enough water to come about halfway up the sides of each wonton crescent. Cover wok with the lid and cook until all the liquid has evaporated, 10 minutes. Remove wontons from wok, cover with foil and keep warm in a preheated 120°C (250°F) Gas ½ oven. Repeat with remaining oil, wonton crescents and water. Serve warm with chilli soy dipping sauce.

THINK AHEAD
Assemble wonton crescents up to 3 hours in advance. Store covered with cling film on a floured oven tray in the refrigerator. Alternatively, freeze (see page 149) up to 1 month in advance. Defrost overnight in the refrigerator. Fry up to 45 minutes before serving. Keep warm, covered in a preheated 120°C (250°F) Gas ½ oven.

COOKS' NOTE
It's the flour that makes the wonton crescents crispy. If assembling ahead of time, dip the wonton crescents again in flour before cooking for maximum crispiness.

For herbed prawn filling, place 75g (2½oz) cooked and peeled prawns, 2 chopped spring onions, 2 tbsp chopped coriander, 1cm (½in) piece ginger, grated, and 1 tbsp fish sauce in food processor or blender; pulse until finely chopped. Fill 1 recipe wonton wrappers or 20 ready made dumpling wrappers as directed by the main recipe. Fry crescents as directed by the main recipe.
For the tangy lime dipping sauce, combine juice of 1 lime with 1 tbsp sugar and 2 tbsp fish sauce. Serve wonton crescents warm with tangy lime dipping sauce.

TEXAS RED BEAN WRAPS WITH CORIANDER CREMA

MAKES 20

FOR BEAN FILLING

2 spring onions
200g (7oz) tin of red kidney beans, drained
1 garlic clove, chopped
¼ tsp Tabasco
juice of 1 lime
salt, black pepper

FOR CREMA

75g (2½oz) cream cheese
15g (½oz) coriander, chopped
1 green chilli, seeded and chopped
½ tbsp olive oil
4 - 20cm (8in) flour tortillas

Roughly chop the white parts of the spring onions. Reserve the green stalks for the crema. For bean filling, place chopped spring onion, beans, garlic, Tabasco and lime in a food processor or blender; pulse until well blended but still retaining some texture. Add salt and pepper to taste. Roughly chop the reserved green stalks of the spring onion. For crema, place chopped spring onion stalks, cream cheese, chilli and oil in a food processor or blender; pulse until smooth.

Heat a dry heavy bottomed frying pan over medium heat. Place 1 tortilla in the pan. Cook until warm, 15 seconds. Flip tortilla over and warm other side, 15 seconds. Remove from pan and cover with a clean tea towel. Repeat with remaining tortillas.

Spread 1 warm tortilla first with 1 tbsp bean filling, then with 1 tbsp crema filling. Roll up tortilla gently, but firmly, as you would a Swiss roll. Wrap securely in cling film (see page 148). Twist the ends to secure. Repeat with remaining tortillas and filling. Refrigerate tortilla rolls 1 hour.

Trim untidy ends with a serrated knife. Cut each tortilla wrap diagonally into 5 slices. Discard the cling film after slicing. Serve chilled or at room temperature.

THINK AHEAD
Make wraps up to 1 day in advance. Refrigerate. Slice up to 1 hour before serving. Discard the cling film just before serving to keep tortilla wraps moist.

COOKS' NOTE
One word of wrap advice, do not overfill. If some filling does ooze out as you roll, simply scrape the excess off with the back of a knife.

ROAST PEPPER, GOAT'S CHEESE AND MINT WRAPS

MAKES 20

1 red pepper, quartered and seeded
4 - 20cm (8in) flour tortillas
75g (2½oz) fresh creamy goat's cheese
15g (½oz) mint, chopped
salt, black pepper

Grill and peel pepper quarters (see page 147). Cut peeled pepper quarters into julienne strips (see page 147).

Heat a dry heavy bottomed frying pan over medium heat. Place 1 tortilla in the pan. Cook until warm, 15 seconds. Flip tortilla over and warm other side, 15 seconds. Remove from pan and cover with a clean tea towel. Repeat with remaining tortillas.

Spread 1 warm tortilla with 1 tbsp goat's cheese. Top with a quarter of the pepper julienne strips. Sprinkle with mint and a pinch each salt and pepper. Roll up tortilla gently but firmly as you would a Swiss roll. Wrap securely in cling film (see page 148). Twist the ends to secure. Repeat with remaining tortillas and filling. Refrigerate tortilla rolls 1 hour.

Trim untidy ends with a serrated knife. Cut each tortilla wrap diagonally into 5 slices. Discard the cling film after slicing. Serve chilled or at room temperature.

THINK AHEAD
Make wraps up to 4 hours in advance. Refrigerate. Slice up to 1 hour before serving. Discard cling film just before serving to keep tortilla wraps moist.

CREPES

MAKES 5

60g (2oz) plain flour
¼ tsp salt
1 egg, beaten
150ml (5floz) milk
30g (1oz) butter

ESSENTIAL EQUIPMENT
23cm (9in) non-stick frying pan

Sift flour and salt into a bowl. Make a
well in the centre and add the egg.
Gradually beat in flour from the sides.
Whisking constantly, slowly pour in
the milk to make a smooth batter.
Cover and let stand at room
temperature for 30 minutes.
Melt butter in the pan over medium
heat. Swirl butter to coat base of pan.
Pour excess melted butter into a bowl
and reserve.
Pour a small ladle of batter into the
pan. Tilt the pan and swirl the batter
to cover the entire base of the pan.
Cook until golden underneath,
1 minute. Flip crepe over with a
rubber spatula and cook until golden
underneath, 30 seconds more.
Remove from pan. Repeat with
reserved butter and remaining batter.
Discard any thick or torn crepes.

THINK AHEAD
Make crepes up to 2 days in advance. Store in
an airtight container stacked in single layers
separated by greaseproof paper. Alternatively,
freeze crepes up to 1 month in advance. Store in
a sealed plastic freezer bag stacked in single
layers separated by plastic wrap (see page 149).
Defrost overnight in refrigerator.

COOKS' NOTE
Be sure to add the milk gradually while whisking
constantly in order to achieve a perfectly smooth
batter. If lumps do occur, pour the batter through
a sieve. Alternatively, make batter in a food
processor or blender; pulse flour, salt, eggs and
milk until smooth.

ROLLED SMOKED HAM CREPES WITH TARRAGON AND MUSTARD CREAM

MAKES 20

125g (4oz) cream cheese
1 tbsp grainy mustard
1 tbsp roughly chopped tarragon leaves
salt, black pepper
1 recipe crepes (see opposite)
5 slices smoked ham

Combine cream cheese, mustard and
tarragon. Add salt and pepper to taste.
Spread crepes with cheese mixture. Roll
up each ham slice tightly. Place 1 tightly
rolled ham slice along the edge of
1 crepe. Roll crepe firmly around ham.
Wrap in cling film. Twist the ends to
secure. Repeat with remaining filling,
ham and crepes. Refrigerate rolls 1 hour.
Trim untidy ends with a serrated knife.
Cut each rolled crepe into 4 slices,
alternating between diagonal and straight
cuts. Discard the cling film after slicing.
Serve chilled or at room temperature.

THINK AHEAD
Make rolled crepes up to 1 day in advance.
Refrigerate. Cut up to 1 hour before serving.

ROLLED RICOTTA AND SAGE CREPES WITH PARMESAN SHAVINGS

MAKES 20

FOR CREPES

60g (2oz) plain flour
¼ tsp salt
1 egg, separated
250ml (8floz) milk
1 tbsp melted butter
1 tbsp finely chopped sage

FOR FILLING

200g (7oz) ricotta cheese
1 tbsp finely chopped sage
1 tbsp finely chopped parsley
1 tbsp grated parmesan cheese
salt, black pepper, nutmeg
60g (2oz) butter
20 parmesan shavings to garnish
(see page 148)

For crepes, place flour, salt, egg yolk,
milk, butter and sage with a pinch of
salt in a food processor or blender; pulse
until smooth. Whisk egg white until soft
peaks form (see page 141). Fold a third
of the batter into the beaten egg white
until lightened. Fold in remaining batter
until well combined. Cover and
refrigerate for 30 minutes.
For filling, combine ricotta, herbs and
parmesan until well combined. Add salt,
pepper and nutmeg to taste.
Melt butter in the pan over a medium
heat. Swirl butter to coat base of pan.
Pour excess melted butter into a bowl
and reserve. Pour a small ladle of batter
into the pan. Tilt the pan and swirl the
batter to cover the entire base of the pan.
Cook until golden underneath, 1 minute.
Flip crepe over with a rubber spatula and
cook until golden underneath, 30 seconds
more. Remove from pan. Repeat with
reserved butter and remaining batter
until used up. Discard any thick or torn
crepes. Cool crepes completely.
Spread ricotta mixture evenly over
crepes. Roll up tightly (see page 148).
Wrap in cling film. Twist the ends to
secure. Refrigerate rolls 1 hour. Trim
untidy ends with a serrated knife. Cut
each rolled crepe into 4 slices. Discard
the cling film after slicing. Garnish with
parmesan shavings. Serve chilled or at
room temperature.

THINK AHEAD
Roll crepes up to 1 day in advance. Cover and
refrigerate. Cut and garnish up to 1 hour before serving.

MINI PEKING DUCK PANCAKES WITH PLUM SAUCE

MAKES 20

1 tsp runny honey
1 tsp light soy sauce
1 duck breast, skinned
4cm (1½in) piece fresh ginger
2 spring onions
½ cucumber, halved and seeded
20 long chives
10 ready-made Chinese pancakes
2 tbsp plum sauce

Preheat oven to 200°C (400°F) Gas 6.
Combine honey and soy. Brush duck with honey soy mixture. Roast duck until browned but still pink and juicy inside, 10 minutes. Cool. Slice duck breast diagonally into 0.5cm (¼n) thick slices.
Cut ginger, spring onions and cucumber in to julienne strips (see page 147). Drop chives into a pan of boiling water. Drain immediately and cool in cold water. Drain and pat dry with kitchen paper.
Cut pancakes in half. Trim a 0.5cm (¼in) strip from the round edge of each pancake half to make 20 straight sided pieces. Spread ¼ tsp plum sauce in centre of each piece. Divide duck slices and julienne strips among pancake strips. Roll up tightly and tie with a chive. Serve at room temperature.

THINK AHEAD
Roast duck breast up to 1 day in advance. Cover and refrigerate. Cut vegetables and blanch chives up to 1 day in advance. Store in an airtight container in the refrigerator. Slice duck and roll pancakes up to 1 hour in advance.

CHIVE-TIED CREPE BUNDLES WITH SMOKED SALMON AND LEMON CREME FRAICHE

MAKES 20

20 long chives
1 recipe crepes (see page 93)
grated zest of 1 lemon
125ml (4floz) crème fraîche
250g (8oz) smoked salmon slices, chopped
2 tbsp finely chopped chives
black pepper
ESSENTIAL EQUIPMENT
8.5cm (3¼in) plain pastry cutter

Drop long chives into a pan of boiling water. Drain and rinse immediately under cold water. Pat dry on kitchen paper. Stamp out 4 rounds from each crepe with the pastry cutter. Combine lemon zest and crème fraîche. Place 1 tsp crème fraîche and 1 tsp smoked salmon in the centre of each crepe round. Sprinkle with chives and a pinch of black pepper. Carefully bring the edges of each crepe together into a little bundle. Tie each bundle with a long chive. Refrigerate until chilled, 15 minutes.

THINK AHEAD
Make crepe bundles up to 4 hours in advance. Store in single layers covered with plastic wrap in the refrigerator.

COOKS' NOTE
To make classic beggars' purses, omit chopped chives and pepper and substitute crème fraîche for sour cream and salmon for black caviar.

HERBED ARTICHOKE AND PARMESAN FILO ROLLS WITH LIGHT LEMON MAYONNAISE DIP

MAKES 20

250g (8oz) artichoke hearts
in oil, drained
100g (3½oz) parmesan cheese,
grated
1 egg, beaten
2 tbsp finely chopped parsley
2 tbsp finely chopped oregano

2 garlic cloves, crushed
¼ tsp salt
¼ tsp black pepper
200g (7oz) filo pastry
45g (1½oz) butter, melted
1 recipe light lemon
mayonnaise (see page 142)

Preheat oven to 180°C (350°F) Gas 4.

For filling, place artichokes, cheese, egg, chopped herbs, garlic, salt and pepper in food processor; pulse until blended. Brush butter on both sides of 3 filo sheets and stack them together. If necessary, trim stacked filo sheets to measure 15cm (6in) in width. Spread 1½ tsp of filling in a thin strip along the short end of the stacked filo. Roll the filo 1½ times around the filling (see below). Brush with butter to seal. Cut along the edge of the roll with a sharp knife to finish. Place the filo roll seam-side down on a buttered baking sheet. Repeat the rolling process with the remaining filling and butter to make about 5 or 6 rolls per filo stack. Layer and butter a new stack of filo sheets when you no longer have room to start a new roll. Repeat buttering and layering with the remaining filo sheets, spreading and rolling with the remaining filling until you have run out of ingredients. Brush finished filo rolls with more butter. Bake until crisp and golden, 15 minutes. Cool on a wire rack. Serve at warm or at room temperature with light lemon mayonnaise for dipping.

THINK AHEAD
Assemble up to 1 day in advance. Store covered in single layers not touching. Alternatively, assemble rolls and freeze up to 1 month in advance (see page 149). Bake from frozen, 20–25 minutes.

COOKS' NOTE
If allowed to dry out, filo pastry becomes brittle and difficult to handle, so be sure to cover with a damp tea towel until ready to use.

MINTED FETA AND PINE NUT FILO ROLLS WITH LEMON AIOLI

MAKES 20

100g (3½oz) pine nuts
100g (3½oz) feta cheese, crumbled
2 tbsp grated parmesan cheese
2 tbsp finely chopped mint
grated zest of ½ lemon

1 tbsp lemon juice
¼ tsp black pepper
30g (1oz) butter, melted
100g (3½oz) filo pastry
1 recipe lemon aioli (see
page 142)

Preheat oven to 180°C (350°F) Gas 4.

For filling, toast pine nuts in a dry pan over a low heat until nutty and golden, 5 minutes. Cool. Place pinenuts, feta, parmesan, mint, lemon zest, lemom juice and pepper in a food processor; pulse until well blended.

Brush butter on both sides of 3 filo sheets and stack them together. If necessary, trim stacked filo sheets to measure 15cm (6in) in width. Spread 2 tsp filling in a thin strip along the short end of the stacked filo. Roll the filo 1½ times around the filling. Brush with butter to seal. Cut along the edge of the roll with a sharp knife to finish, then cut the finished roll in half. Place the 2 filo rolls seam-side down on a buttered baking sheet. Repeat the rolling process with the remaining filling and butter to make about 10 or 12 rolls per filo stack. Layer and butter a new stack of filo sheets when you no longer have room to start a new roll. Repeat buttering and layering with the remaining filo sheets, spreading and rolling with the remaining filling until you have run out of ingredients.

Brush filo rolls with butter. Bake until crisp and golden, 15 minutes. Cool on a wire rack. Serve at warm or at room temperature, with lemon aioli for dipping.

THINK AHEAD
Assemble up to 1 day in advance. Store covered in single layers not touching and refrigerate. Alternatively, assemble rolls and freeze up to 1 month in advance (see page 149). Bake from frozen, 20–25 minutes.

FILO TARTLETS

MAKES 20
75g (2½oz) filo pastry
2 tbsp melted butter
ESSENTIAL EQUIPMENT
pastry brush, 2 - 12-cup mini muffin tins

Preheat oven to 180°C (350°F) Gas 4. Brush one sheet of filo pastry with the melted butter (see opposite, top). With a sharp knife cut into 5cm x 5cm (2in x 2in) squares (see opposite, middle). Butter the muffin cups and line each one with 3 buttered filo pastry squares placed at slightly different angles (see opposite, bottom). Repeat until all the filo pastry has been used. Bake to a deep golden brown, 6 to 8 minutes. Carefully remove the tartlets from the cups and leave to cool completely on a wire rack.

THINK AHEAD
Bake tartlets up to 1 month in advance. Store in an airtight container at room temperature.

COOKS' NOTE
To prevent the filo pastry from drying out, cover with a damp cloth until ready to use. If the buttered filo sticks to your fingers, use the pastry brush to press the filo squares into the muffin cups.

FILO TARTLETS WITH BANG BANG CHICKEN

MAKES 20
2 tbsp sesame seeds
4 tbsp smooth peanut butter
1 garlic clove, crushed
5cm (2in) piece fresh ginger, chopped
2 tbsp lemon juice
1 tbsp dark soy sauce
¼ tsp Tabasco
1 boneless, skinless chicken breast
1 recipe filo tartlets (see above)
1 spring onion, finely sliced on the diagonal (see below, right)

Preheat oven to 180°C (350°F) Gas 4.
Toast seeds in a dry pan over low heat until nutty and golden, 3 minutes. Mix peanut butter, garlic, ginger, lemon, soy and Tabasco to a smooth sauce.
Put chicken in pan with cold water to cover. Bring slowly to simmering point. Simmer gently without boiling until cooked through, 7 to 10 minutes. Cool completely in cooking liquid. Drain and cut chicken on the diagonal into 0.25cm (⅛in) thick slices. Cut slices in half. Place 1 tsp bang bang sauce in each tartlet. Arrange chicken slices on top. Sprinkle over toasted seeds.
Garnish with spring onion slices.

THINK AHEAD
Make sauce up to 3 days in advance. Cover and refrigerate. Cook chicken up to 1 day in advance. Cover and refrigerate. Fill tartlets up to 45 minutes before serving.

SLICING SPRING ONION
Trim spring onion at both ends. Finely slice green stem at an angle to make sharp spikes.

FILO TARTLETS WITH SMOKED SALMON, CRACKED PEPPER AND LIME

MAKES 20

150g (5oz) smoked salmon slices
1 lime, peeled and segmented (see page 147)
125ml (4floz) crème fraîche
1 recipe filo tartlets (see page 98)
juice of 1 lime
½ tsp cracked black peppercorns
15g (½oz) chives, cut into 2cm (¾in) spikes

Cut salmon slices into thin strips, 0.5cm (¼in) wide. Cut lime segments into 1cm (½in) pieces. Place 1 tsp crème fraîche in base of each tartlet. Top with smoked salmon strips. Spoon over a few drops of lime juice and sprinkle with cracked black pepper. Garnish with lime segments and chive spikes.

THINK AHEAD
Fill tartlets up to 45 minutes before serving.

COOKS' NOTE
You can buy cracked black pepper, but it is easy to make yourself. Crush the peppercorns in a mortar with a pestle until cracked to tiny pieces rather than ground to a powder.

FILO TARTLETS WITH SMOKED CHICKEN, BLACK OLIVES AND PARSLEY PESTO

MAKES 20

15g (½oz) parsley
1 clove garlic, crushed
4 tbsp pine nuts
4 tbsp parmesan cheese, grated
juice of ½ lemon
2 tbsp olive oil
salt, black pepper
1 smoked chicken breast
1 recipe filo tartlets (see page 98)
10 stoned black olives, halved

Place parsley, garlic, pine nuts, parmesan, lemon juice and oil in a food processor or blender; pulse to a thick paste. Add salt and pepper to taste. Cut chicken into thin strips, 0.5cm (¼in) wide. Put 1 tsp pesto into each tartlet. Arrange chicken strips on top. Garnish with half an olive. Serve at room temperature.

THINK AHEAD
Make pesto up to 3 days in advance. Cover and refrigerate. Fill tartlets up to 45 minutes before serving.

FILO TARTLETS WITH CRAB, GINGER AND LIME

MAKES 20
1 tbsp sesame seeds
250g (¾ lb) white crab meat
2.5cm (1in) piece fresh ginger,
finely chopped
juice of 2 limes
15g (½oz) coriander, leaves stripped
¼ red pepper, cut into strips
4 tbsp mayonnaise (see page 142)
salt, Tabasco
1 recipe filo tartlets (see page 98)
1 lime, peeled and segmented
(see page 147)

Toast seeds in a dry pan over low heat until golden brown, 3 minutes. Toss crab with ginger, lime, coriander, pepper, mayonnaise and toasted seeds. Add salt and Tabasco to taste. Cut lime segments into 1cm (½in) pieces. Divide crab among filo tartlets. Garnish with lime segments. Serve at room temperature.

THINK AHEAD
Make filling up to 1 day in advance but only add coriander up to 1 hour before serving.

FILO TARTLETS WITH SPICY CORIANDER PRAWNS

MAKES 20
2 tsp sesame seeds
125g (4oz) medium prawns, cooked
and peeled
15g (½oz) coriander, chopped
6 tbsp Thai sweet chilli sauce
1 recipe filo tartlets (see page 98)

Toast seeds in a dry pan over low heat until golden brown, 3 minutes. Combine prawns, coriander and chilli sauce. Spoon into tartlets and garnish with toasted seeds.

THINK AHEAD
Make filling up to 1 day in advance. Cover and refrigerate. Fill tartlets up to 45 minutes before serving.

COOKS' NOTE
If using frozen cooked prawns, defrost in a colander. When defrosted, squeeze out water with your hands and pat dry with kitchen paper.

FILO TARTLETS WITH ASIAN BEEF SALAD

MAKES 20
200g (7oz) beef fillet steak, 2.5cm
(1in) thick
1 tbsp light soy sauce
1 tbsp lime juice
1 tbsp fish sauce
¼ tsp sugar
15g (½oz) coriander, leaves stripped
15g (½oz) mint, leaves stripped
¼ red pepper, finely diced
1 tomato, seeded and diced (see page 147)
1 tsp sesame seeds
1 tsp grated lime zest
1 recipe filo tartlets (see page 98)
1 sliced red chilli to garnish

Sear steak in hot pan on both sides, 6 minutes in total. Cool and cut into 20 slices. Toss steak slices with soy, lime, fish sauce, sugar, fresh herbs, pepper, tomato, seeds and zest. Divide steak slices among filo tartlets. Garnish with red chilli.

THINK AHEAD
Make filling up to 1 day in advance, but only add fresh herbs up to 1 hour before serving. Cover and refrigerate. Fill tartlets up to 45 minutes before serving.

CORN CUPS

MAKES 20
125g (4oz) masa harina (see page 163)
½ tsp salt
150ml (5floz) warm water

ESSENTIAL EQUIPMENT
6.5cm (2½in) plain pastry cutter,
2 - 12-cup mini muffin tins

Preheat oven to 200°C (400°F) Gas 6.
Place masa harina and salt in a bowl.
Pour in water and mix with a fork to
form a rough dough. Turn out onto a
clean surface and knead until smooth
and firm, 1 minute. Roll into a
smooth ball, cover with a tea towel
and let rest for 30 minutes.
Cut dough in half. Roll out 1 piece of
dough between 2 pieces of cling film
to a 2mm (⅛in) thickness. Peel off
the top layer of cling film. Stamp out
10 rounds with the pastry cutter.
Line 10 oiled muffin cups with the
rounds. Repeat with remaining
dough and muffin cups. Bake until
crisp and dry, 20 minutes. Cool on a
wire rack.

THINK AHEAD
Bake cups up to 3 days in advance. Store in an
airtight container at room temperature.

COOKS' NOTE
Corn dough is an easy-going, malleable dough to
work with. If the dough should tear slightly as
you line the muffin cups, simply patch up by
pressing over with a scrap of dough.

CORN CUPS WITH PAPAYA, AVOCADO AND PINK GRAPEFRUIT SALAD

MAKES 20
½ pink grapefruit, peeled and segmented
(see page 147)
½ papaya
½ red onion, finely chopped
1 red chilli, seeded and finely chopped
2 tbsp finely chopped mint
1 tbsp red wine vinegar
2 tbsp sunflower oil
1 small avocado, quartered
salt, black pepper
1 recipe corn cups (see opposite)

Cut each grapefruit segment into
1cm (½in) pieces. Cut papaya half into
quarters. Cut each papaya quarter into
fine slices. Combine grapefruit, papaya,
onion, chilli, mint, vinegar and oil. Cut
each avocado quarter into fine slices.
Add to salad and gently combine.
Add salt and pepper to taste. Divide
among corn cups. Serve chilled or at
room temperature.

THINK AHEAD
Make salad up to 8 hours in advance, but add mint
not more than 3 hours in advance for best colour.
Press cling film directly on to the surface of the salad
and refrigerate. Fill corn cups just before serving.

CORN CUPS WITH TUNA, MANGO AND LIME CEVICHE

MAKES 20
175g (6oz) fresh tuna
juice of 2 limes
1 green chilli, seeded and finely diced
½ medium red onion, finely chopped
1 mango, finely diced
2 tbsp finely chopped coriander
1 tsp salt
1 recipe corn cups (see opposite)

Cut tuna into fine dice. Combine tuna
and lime in a non-metallic bowl. Cover
and refrigerate, stirring occasionally, for
3 hours. Drain, discarding all but 1 tbsp
marinade. Combine tuna, chilli, onion,
mango, coriander, salt and reserved
1 tbsp marinade. Divide among corn
cups. Serve chilled.

THINK AHEAD
Make ceviche up to 1 day in advance, but add
coriander not more than 3 hours before serving for
best colour. Cover and refrigerate. Fill corn cups just
before serving.

COOKS' NOTE
Fresh salmon, halibut and scallops all make
excellent ceviche. If you are uncomfortable about
serving raw fish, use cooked, peeled prawns instead.

CLAMS WITH GINGER AND LIME BUTTER

MAKES 20
90g (3oz) butter, softened
1cm (½in) piece fresh ginger,
finely chopped
grated zest and juice of 1 lime
1 tbsp finely chopped coriander
salt, black pepper
20 clams
6 tbsp coarse salt

Combine butter, ginger, lime and coriander. Add salt and pepper to taste. Scrub clams under running water. Discard any that are broken or not tightly closed.
Place clams in a pan with 2 tbsp water and cover with lid. Steam over medium heat until open, 6 minutes. Shake pan occasionally to ensure even cooking. Remove clams with a slotted spoon. Discard any that are shut. Cool. Prise open with your fingers. Discard top shells. Loosen clams from bottom shells. Sprinkle a heatproof serving dish evenly with salt. Arrange half shells on salt. Divide butter among clams. Before serving, place clams under a preheated grill until butter melts, 2 minutes. Serve hot.

THINK AHEAD
Make butter up to 1 week in advance. Cover and refrigerate. Cook clams up to 1 day in advance. Cover and refrigerate. Top clams with butter up to 1 hour in advance. Grill and serve hot.

COOKS' NOTE
To barbecue clams, place unopened on a grill set 15cm (6in) above hot coals. When the shells open, the clams are done, 5 minutes. Discard top shell. Have the ginger and lime butter already melted and drizzle over the cooked clams. Cool slightly before serving or you might burn your fingers.

BACON-WRAPPED OYSTERS

MAKES 20
20 fresh oysters
200g (7oz) sliced streaky bacon with the rind removed
1½ tbsp Worcestershire sauce
20 tbsp coarse salt

ESSENTIAL EQUIPMENT
20 wooden toothpicks

Preheat oven to 200°C (400°F) Gas 6. Open the oysters (see below), reserving 20 bottom shells for serving.
Cut bacon slices across into 20 strips, each 4cm (1¾in) long. Wrap a bacon strip around each oyster and secure with a toothpick. Place wrapped oysters on a baking sheet. Bake until bacon is lightly coloured and cooked through, 10 minutes. Arrange oysters on reserved shells. To make a stable base for serving the oyster, place each half shell on 1 tbsp of coarse salt. Sprinkle oysters with Worcestershire sauce. Serve hot.

THINK AHEAD
Wrap oysters in bacon up to 2 hours in advance. Cover and refrigerate.

OPENING OYSTERS
Hold oyster flat side up in a tea towel. Insert a short, wide-bladed kitchen or oyster knife into hinge of the oyster and twist to prise shell open. Scrape oyster free from top shell. Slice under flesh to detach oyster from bottom shell.

MUSSELS WITH SALSA CRUDA

MAKES 20
20 large fresh mussels
6 tbsp coarse sea salt
2 tomatoes, peeled, seeded and diced (see page 147)
1 green chilli, seeded and finely chopped
½ medium red onion, finely chopped
2 tbsp olive oil
1 tbsp lime juice
salt, black pepper

Scrub mussels under running water. Discard any that are broken or not tightly closed. Pull off their beards with your fingers. Place mussels in a pan with 2 tbsp water and cover with lid. Steam over medium heat until open, 6 minutes. Shake pan occasionally to ensure even cooking. Remove mussels with a slotted spoon. Discard any that are shut. Cool. Prise open with your fingers. Discard top shells. Loosen mussels from bottom shells. Sprinkle serving dish evenly with coarse salt. Arrange mussels in half shells on salt. For salsa, combine tomatoes, chilli, onion, lime and oil. Add salt and pepper to taste. Spoon over mussels. Serve at room temperature or chilled.

THINK AHEAD
Cook mussels up to 1 day in advance. Cover and refrigerate. Make salsa up to 5 hours in advance. Cover and refrigerate. Top mussels up to 30 minutes before serving.

EGG AND BACON PUFFS

MAKES 35
200g (7oz) streaky bacon rashers
1 hardboiled egg, halved
4 tbsp mayonnaise (see page 142)
15g (½oz) chives, finely sliced
salt, black pepper
1 recipe baked choux puffs
(see pages 138–139)

Preheat oven to 180°C (350°F) Gas 4.
Place bacon rashers on a foil-lined
baking sheet. Bake until golden and
crisp, about 10–15 minutes. Drain bacon
on kitchen paper, then cut into small
dice. Separate egg yolk from white. Cut
white into fine dice. Crush yolk with
fork. Combine bacon, white, mayonnaise
and chives (reserving 2 tsp chives for
garnish). Add salt and pepper to taste.
Cut 0.5cm (¼in) slice from the top of
each puff with a serrated knife. Spoon
egg and bacon mixture into puffs.
Sprinkle with egg yolk. Garnish with
chives. Serve at room temperature
or chilled.

THINK AHEAD
Make filling up to 1 day in advance. Cover and
refrigerate. Fill puffs up to 3 hours in advance.
Refrigerate. Garnish up to 45 minutes before serving.

CLASSIC PRAWN COCKTAIL PUFFS

MAKES 35
200g (7oz) small prawns, cooked
and peeled
3 tbsp mayonnaise (see page 142)
1 tbsp tomato ketchup
1 tsp Worcestershire sauce
salt, Tabasco
1 recipe baked choux puffs
(see pages 138–139)
2 little gem lettuces or romaine hearts,
separated into leaves
paprika to garnish

Combine prawns, mayonnaise, ketchup
and Worcestershire sauce. Add salt and
Tabasco to taste. Cut 0.5cm (¼in) slice
from top of each puff with a serrated
knife. Cut stalks from salad leaves and
discard. Cut each leaf into 2.5cm (1in)
pieces. Tuck one lettuce piece into each
puff. Spoon prawn mixture on top.
Dust with paprika. Serve at room
temperature or chilled.

THINK AHEAD
Make filling up to 1 day in advance. Cover and
refrigerate. Fill puffs up to 3 hours in advance.
Refrigerate. Garnish up to 45 minutes before serving.

LIGHT LEMONY SALMON MOUSSE PUFFS

MAKES 35
200g (7oz) salmon fillet
2 tbsp cream cheese
2 tsp horseradish sauce
2 tsp lemon juice
salt, white pepper
150ml (5floz) whipping cream
1 recipe baked choux puffs
(see pages 138–139)
100g (3½oz) salmon caviar
35 dill sprigs to garnish

ESSENTIAL EQUIPMENT
piping bag with large star nozzle

Place salmon in pan of boiling water.
When water returns to a boil, remove
from heat at once. Leave salmon in
water to cool completely. Drain on
kitchen paper. Place salmon with cream
cheese, horseradish and lemon in a food
processor or blender; pulse until smooth.
Be careful not to over mix. Add salt and
pepper to taste. Whip cream until it
holds soft peaks (see page 144). Gently
fold salmon mixture into cream.
Cut 0.5cm (¼in) slice from the top of
each puff using a serrated knife. Fill
piping bag with mousse (see page 146).
Pipe mousse into puffs. Garnish with
salmon caviar and dill sprigs. Serve
chilled or at room temperature.

THINK AHEAD
Make filling up to 3 hours in advance. Cover and
refrigerate. Fill and garnish up to 1 hour in advance.

CARAMEL PROFITEROLES

MAKES 35

4 tbsp caster sugar

2 tbsp water

500ml (16floz) vanilla ice cream

1 recipe baked choux puffs (see pages 138–139)

ESSENTIAL EQUIPMENT

baking sheet lined with oiled baking parchment, melon baller

Put sugar and water in small pan and stir to dissolve. Bring to boil over medium heat. Cook to a light caramel (see page 145 and below, left). Dip each puff in caramel (see below, right). Place puffs dipped side down on the prepared baking sheet. Allow the caramel to set. Cut each dipped choux in half with a serrated knife.

With melon baller, scoop up 1 ball of ice cream. Sandwich the ice cream ball between 2 halves of 1 choux puff. Repeat with remaining ice cream and puffs. Serve immediately.

THINK AHEAD

Dip puffs up to 3 hours in advance.

MINI ECLAIRS

MAKES 30

1 recipe baked choux mini éclairs (see pages 138–139)

1 recipe chocolate pastry cream (see page 145)

100g (3½oz) chocolate

Pierce a small hole in underside of each éclair. Fill piping bag with pastry cream (see page 146). Pipe cream into pierced hole in each éclair (see below, left). Melt chocolate (see page 145). Remove from hot water. Hold base of each éclair between finger and thumb. Dip each éclair's upper surface in to the chocolate. Remove quickly and allow excess chocolate to drip off (see below, right). Place on a wire rack, until chocolate is set. Serve cold or at room temperature.

THINK AHEAD

Fill and dip up to 1 day in advance. Cover and refrigerate. Alternatively, bake and freeze mini choux éclairs up to 3 weeks in advance. Crisp from frozen in a preheated 180°C (350°F) Gas 4 oven for 3 minutes. Cool completely before filling and dipping.

COOK TO A LIGHT CARAMEL

DIP EACH PUFF IN CARAMEL

FILLING ECLAIRS

DIPPING ECLAIRS

CROUSTADES

MAKES 20

7 thin slices white bread
2 tbsp melted butter

ESSENTIAL EQUIPMENT

1 rolling pin, 1 - 5cm (2in) fluted pastry
cutter, 2 - 12-cup muffin tins

Preheat oven to 200°C (400°F) Gas 6.
Roll out bread slices thinly with the
rolling pin. Stamp out 3 rounds from
each slice using the pastry cutter. Line
each hole of 1 muffin tin with a bread
round. Brush each round with butter.
Press the empty muffin tin on top.
Bake until golden brown and crisp,
10 minutes. Repeat with remaining
bread.

THINK AHEAD
Make up to 3 days in advance. Store in an airtight
container at room temperature.

COOKS' NOTE
Put your pasta machine to unusual but most efficacious
use by rolling out the bread in it. Set machine on the
third setting and roll the bread slices through twice.
Stamp out rounds according to the recipe.

MINI CAESAR SALAD CROUSTADES

MAKES 20

2 romaine hearts, leaves separated
2 tbsp mayonnaise (see page 142)
dash of Worcestershire sauce
squeeze of lemon juice
5 drained anchovy fillets, finely chopped
1 tbsp parmesan cheese, grated
1 recipe croustades (see opposite)
20 parmesan shavings to garnish
(see page 148)

Stack salad leaves and roll up tightly.
Slice across roll to make 0.5cm (¼in)
strips. Flavour mayonnaise with
Worcestershire sauce and lemon juice.
Toss salad with mayonnaise, anchovies
and grated parmesan. Fill croustades
with salad. Garnish with parmesan
shavings.

THINK AHEAD
Prepare salad leaves up to 1 day in advance. Store
in an airtight container in the refrigerator. Fill
croustades up to 1 hour before serving.

TOMATO CONCASSEE WITH CREME FRAICHE AND CHIVES CROUSTADES

MAKES 20

3 ripe tomatoes, peeled, seeded and diced
(see page 147)
2 tbsp finely chopped chives
2 tbsp crème fraîche
2 tbsp lemon juice
Tabasco
salt, black pepper
1 recipe croustades (see opposite)

Combine tomatoes with chives, crème
fraîche, lemon and a dash of Tabasco.
Cover and refrigerate for 1 hour. Add
salt and pepper to taste. Spoon
concassée into croustades. Serve cold.

THINK AHEAD
Make concassée the day before, but only add salt
and pepper just before using. Store in an airtight
container in the refrigerator. Fill croustades up to
45 minutes before serving.

POACHED SALMON WITH DILL MAYONNAISE CROUSTADES

MAKES 20
300g (10oz) salmon fillet
1 recipe croustades (see page 108)
salt, white pepper
6 tbsp mayonnaise (see page 142)
2 tbsp finely chopped dill
20 dill sprigs to garnish

Place salmon in pan of boiling water. When water returns to boil, remove from heat at once and leave to cool completely. Drain salmon on kitchen paper. Separate into large flakes. Divide salmon among croustades. Sprinkle with salt and white pepper. Combine mayonnaise and dill. Spoon mayonnaise over salmon. Garnish with dill sprigs. Serve at room temperature.

THINK AHEAD
Cook salmon up to 3 days in advance. Cover and refrigerate. Fill croustades up to 45 minutes before serving.

COOKS' NOTE
Use very finely chopped coriander and a squeeze of lime in place of dill to create a subtle oriental flavour.

QUAIL EGG, CAVIAR AND CHERVIL CROUSTADES

MAKES 20
10 quail eggs
6 tbsp mayonnaise (see page 142)
1 recipe croustades (see page 108)
100g (3½oz) black lumpfish caviar
100g (3½oz) red lumpfish caviar
20 sprigs of chervil or parsley to garnish

Cook quail eggs in pan of boiling water for 10 minutes. Drain and refresh in cold water. Peel and cut in half. Spoon mayonnaise into croustades. Place half a quail egg cut side up on top of the mayonnaise. Top with ½ tsp each black and red caviar. Garnish with herb sprigs. Serve at room temperature.

THINK AHEAD
Cook and peel eggs up to 2 days in advance. Cover with water and refrigerate. Fill croustades up to 45 minutes before serving.

COOKS' NOTE
As an alternative filling, try quail eggs with lemon hollandaise (see page 143), crispy crumbled bacon and snipped chives.

USING A ZESTER
Press down lightly, drag or pull the zester across the lemon rind.

CHICKEN TONNATO WITH LEMON AND CAPERS CROUSTADES

MAKES 20
1 boneless, skinless chicken breast
2 tbsp drained tuna
2 drained anchovy fillets
2 tbsp mayonnaise (see page 142)
1 tsp lemon juice
salt, black pepper
1 recipe croustades (see page 108)
20 drained capers
zest of ½ lemon to garnish (see below)

ESSENTIAL EQUIPMENT
zester

Put chicken in pan with cold water to cover. Bring slowly to a simmer over medium-low heat. Simmer gently without boiling until cooked through, 7 to 10 minutes. Cool completely in cooking liquid. Drain and cut chicken into fine dice. For tonnato sauce, place tuna, anchovies, mayonnaise and lemon in a food processor; pulse until smooth. Add salt and pepper to taste. Divide chicken among croustades. Spoon over sauce. Garnish with capers and lemon zest. Serve at room temperature.

THINK AHEAD
Make tonnato sauce up to 3 days in advance. Cover and refrigerate. Cook chicken up to 1 day in advance. Cover and refrigerate. Fill croustades up to 45 minutes before serving.

CARROT, HONEY AND GINGER SOUP CUPS

MAKES 20

30g (1oz) butter
750g (1½ lb) carrots, chopped
1 onion, chopped
1 garlic clove, chopped
10cm (4in) piece fresh ginger, chopped
3 celery sticks, chopped
salt, black pepper
1 litre (1¾ pints) chicken stock
1 tbsp honey
4 tbsp double cream
1 tbsp chopped chives to garnish

ESSENTIAL EQUIPMENT
20 espresso or demi-tasse cups

Melt butter in a pan over low heat. Add carrots, onion, garlic, ginger and celery with a pinch of salt. Continue cooking covered until very soft, 20 minutes. Add stock and increase heat to boil. Reduce heat and simmer until carrots are cooked through, 15 minutes. Cool slightly, then place in a food processor or blender; pulse to a smooth purée. Place a fine-mesh sieve over the rinsed out pan and push the purée through. Discard bits left behind. Add 30ml (1floz) water to the purée at a time to adjust the soup's thickness to a sipping consistency. Heat soup through over a medium heat. Add honey, cream, salt and pepper to taste. Ladle into cups. Sprinkle with chives to garnish. Serve hot.

THINK AHEAD
Make up to 2 days in advance. Cover and refrigerate.

COOK'S NOTE
Remember that this soup will be sipped from a cup and not served with a spoon. Add water as specified by the recipe to achieve the proper consistency for this.

CHILLED SPICED CHICKPEA SOUP CUPS WITH AVOCADO SALSA

MAKES 20

FOR SOUP
400g (14oz) tin of chickpeas, drained
400g (14oz) tin of tomatoes
125ml (4floz) Greek-style yoghurt
2 garlic cloves, crushed
1 tsp ground cumin
1 tbsp lemon juice
2 tbsp olive oil
salt, cayenne pepper

FOR SALSA
1 medium avocado
½ medium red onion, finely chopped
1 tbsp finely chopped mint
1 tbsp lemon juice
1 tbsp olive oil
salt, black pepper
6 tbsp Greek-style yoghurt

ESSENTIAL EQUIPMENT
20 espresso or demi-tasse cups

For soup, place chickpeas, tomatoes, yoghurt, garlic, cumin, lemon and oil in a food processor or blender; pulse to a smooth purée. Transfer purée to a bowl. Gradually add up to 125ml (4floz) water to adjust the soup's thickness to a sipping consistency. Add salt and pepper to taste. Cover and refrigerate for 30 minutes to allow flavours to blend.
For salsa, cut avocado into fine dice. Combine avocado, onion, mint, lime and oil. Add salt and pepper to taste. Cover and refrigerate for 15 minutes to allow flavours to blend. Ladle soup into cups. Top with 1 tsp each salsa and sour cream. Serve chilled.

THINK AHEAD
Make soup up to 2 days in advance. Cover and refrigerate. Make salsa up to 8 hours in advance. Cover tightly with cling film and refrigerate.

COOKS' NOTE
To help keep the salsa from discolouring when making it in advance, press a piece of cling film directly on to the surface of the salsa. It's the oxygen in the air that turns peeled avocado brown, so the less air that comes into contact with the salsa, the longer it will stay looking fresh.

FOCACCINE FARCITE WITH WILD MUSHROOMS AND THYME

MAKES 20

1 tbsp olive oil
2 shallots, finely chopped
100g (3½oz) wild mushrooms, roughly chopped
1 tsp finely chopped thyme
salt, black pepper
1 recipe unbaked bread dough
(see page 140)
1 tsp coarse salt
3 thyme sprigs, roughly chopped

ESSENTIAL EQUIPMENT
5cm (2in) plain pastry cutter

Preheat oven to 200°C (400°F) Gas 6. Heat oil in a frying pan. Add shallots and mushrooms. Stir-fry over high heat until softened, 5 minutes. Add chopped thyme, salt and pepper to taste. Cool completely. Roll out dough to a 0.25cm (⅛in) thickness. Stamp out 40 rounds with pastry cutter. Place 20 dough rounds on to a floured baking sheet. Spoon over wild mushrooms. Top with remaining dough rounds. Press edges down to seal. Sprinkle with coarse salt. Bake until crisp and golden, 15 minutes. Garnish with thyme sprigs and serve warm.

THINK AHEAD
Bake focaccine up to 1 day in advance. Store in an airtight container. Crisp for 10 minutes in preheated 200°C (400°F) Gas 6 oven. Freeze unbaked (see page 149) for up to 1 month in advance. Bake from frozen in preheated 200°C (400°F) Gas 6 oven for 20 minutes.

FOCACCINE FARCITE WITH RAISINS, FENNEL AND GRAPES

MAKES 20

100g (3½oz) raisins
1 recipe unbaked bread dough
(see page 140)
30 black or red grapes, halved
2 tbsp fennel seeds

ESSENTIAL EQUIPMENT
5cm (2in) plain pastry cutter

Preheat oven to 200°C (400°F) Gas 6. Pour boiling water to cover over raisins and leave to soak until plump, 30 minutes. Drain and discard water. Roll out dough to a 0.25cm (⅛in) thickness. Stamp out 40 rounds with the pastry cutter. Place 20 dough rounds on floured baking sheet. Cover with raisins and top with remaining dough rounds. Press edges down to seal. Top each focaccina with 3 grape halves and sprinkle with fennel seeds. Bake until crisp and golden, 15 minutes. Serve warm.

THINK AHEAD
Bake focaccine up to 1 day in advance. Store in an airtight container. Crisp for 10 minutes in preheated 200°C (400°F) Gas 6 oven and serve warm. Freeze unbaked (see page 149) for up to 1 month in advance. Bake from frozen in preheated 200°C (400°F) Gas 6 oven for 20 minutes.

FOCACCINE FARCITE WITH BLUE CHEESE AND ROCKET

MAKES 20

1 recipe unbaked bread dough
(see page 140)
125g (4oz) gorgonzola cheese, crumbled
15g (½oz) rocket leaves
2 tomatoes, seeded and diced
(see page 147)
salt, black pepper
1 tbsp olive oil

ESSENTIAL EQUIPMENT
5cm (2in) plain pastry cutter

Preheat oven to 200°C (400°F) Gas 6. Roll out dough to a 0.25cm (⅛in) thickness. Stamp out 40 rounds with the pastry cutter. Place 20 dough rounds on to a floured baking sheet. Top each focaccina with 1 teaspoon cheese, 2 rocket leaves and ½ tsp diced tomato. Sprinkle with salt and pepper. Place remaining dough rounds on top. Press edges down to seal. Dimple focaccine with your fingertips. Bake until crisp and golden, 15 minutes. Brush with olive oil and serve warm.

THINK AHEAD
Bake focaccine up to 1 day in advance. Store in an airtight container. Crisp for 10 minutes in preheated 200°C (400°F) Gas 6 oven and serve warm. Freeze unbaked (see page 149) for up to 1 month in advance. Bake from frozen in preheated 200°C (400°F) Gas 6 oven for 20 minutes.

MINI DOUBLE CHOCOLATE MERINGUE KISSES

MAKES 20

100g (3½ oz) chocolate
100ml (3½ floz) whipping cream
1 tbsp caster sugar
1 recipe chocolate meringue kisses
(see page 141)
2 tsp cocoa powder to dust

Melt chocolate (see page 145); cool. Whip cream until it holds soft peaks. Whisk in caster sugar (see page 144). Hold 1 meringue by its pointed end and dip its flat underside in chocolate; repeat with another meringue. Sandwich two prepared meringues together with 1 tsp cream in between. Repeat with remaining meringues. Dust with cocoa powder. Serve at room temperature.

THINK AHEAD
Fill kisses up 2 hours in advance. Keep at room temperature until ready to serve.

MINI RASPBERRY RIPPLE MERINGUE KISSES

MAKES 20

100ml (3½ floz) whipping cream
1 tbsp caster sugar
100g (3½ oz) raspberries
1 recipe vanilla meringue kisses
(see page 141)

Whip cream until it holds soft peaks. Whisk in caster sugar (see page 144). Crush raspberries with fork and gently fold into cream until cream is "rippled" with raspberry colour. Hold 1 meringue by its pointed end and scoop up a little of the raspberry cream on its flat underside; repeat with another meringue. Sandwich two prepared meringues together. Repeat with remaining meringues. Refrigerate for 30 minutes to set cream. Serve chilled.

THINK AHEAD
Fill kisses up to 3 hours in advance. Cover and refrigerate.

MINI LEMON MERINGUE KISSES

MAKES 20

100ml (3½ floz) whipping cream
1 tbsp caster sugar
4 tbsp lemon curd
1 recipe vanilla meringue kisses
(see page 141)
2 tsp icing sugar to dust

Whip cream until it holds soft peaks. Whisk in caster sugar (see page 144). Fold lemon curd into whipped cream. Hold 1 meringue by its pointed end and scoop up a little of the lemon cream on its flat underside; repeat with another meringue. Sandwich two prepared meringues together. Repeat with remaining meringues. Refrigerate for 30 minutes to set cream. Dust with icing sugar to garnish. Serve chilled.

THINK AHEAD
Fill kisses up to 3 hours in advance. Cover and refrigerate. Dust with sugar just before serving.

MINI BURGER BUNS

MAKES 25

**1 recipe unbaked bread dough
(see page 140)
1 egg yolk beaten with 1 tbsp water
1 tbsp sesame seeds**

Preheat oven to 200°C (400°F) Gas 6.
Divide dough into small walnut-sized
pieces and shape into smooth rolls.
Place on a floured baking sheet and
press down gently to flatten to buns.
Cover with a cloth and leave for 20
minutes until doubled in size. Brush
each bun with beaten egg and
sprinkle with sesame seeds. Bake
until golden brown, 10 minutes.
Cool on a wire rack.

THINK AHEAD
Bake buns up to 3 days in advance. Store in an
airtight container at room temperature. Alternatively,
shape and freeze buns. Bake frozen buns in
preheated 200°C (400°F) Gas 6 oven for 20 minutes.

COOKS' NOTE
No time for bread-making? Buy full-size burger
buns and cut in half. Stamp out rounds using a
4cm (1½ in) pastry cutter from each half.

MINI HAMBURGERS WITH PICKLES AND KETCHUP

MAKES 25

**300g (10oz) minced beef
1 tbsp very finely chopped onion
2 tbsp Worcestershire sauce
1 tsp creamy Dijon mustard
1 tsp salt, ¼ tsp black pepper
4 tbsp tomato ketchup
1 recipe mini burger buns, halved
(see opposite)
2 little gem lettuces or romaine hearts,
separated into leaves
10 cornichons, to garnish**

Preheat oven to 200°C (400°F) Gas 6.
Mix beef, onion, Worcestershire sauce,
mustard, salt and pepper and 1 tbsp
ketchup until well combined. Divide
mixture into 25 walnut-sized pieces.
With wet hands, shape pieces into balls
and flatten into burgers. Place on baking
sheet and cook until browned and firm
to the touch, 10 minutes. Cut stalks
from salad leaves and discard. Cut
leaves into 2.5cm (1in) pieces. Cut
cornichons on diagonal into thin slices.
Place burgers on bottom halves of
burger buns. Top with salad, cornichon
slices and ketchup. Gently press on top
half of burger bun. Serve warm or at
room temperature.

THINK AHEAD
Cut buns up to 1 day in advance. Store in an airtight
container at room temperature. Shape burgers up to
1 day in advance. Cover and refrigerate. Assemble
burgers up to 3 hours in advance.

COOKS' NOTE
When shaping the burgers, take care to flatten them
properly. If the mini burgers have a slightly domed
top, the burger buns will tend to topple off.

MINI TUNA BURGERS WITH WASABI MAYONNAISE AND PICKLED GINGER

MAKES 25

**250g (8oz) tuna steak, 1.5cm (½in) thick
4 tbsp mayonnaise (see page 142)
1 tsp wasabi paste
¼ tsp soy sauce
¼ tsp rice vinegar
pinch sugar
25 pieces pickled ginger
25 coriander leaves to garnish
1 recipe mini burger buns, halved and
toasted (see opposite)**

ESSENTIAL EQUIPMENT
cast-iron grill pan.

Cut tuna into 2.5cm (1in) cubes.
Preheat pan over a high heat. Sear tuna
cubes on both sides until firm to touch,
2 minutes per side. Add salt and pepper
to taste. Cool.
Combine mayonnaise, wasabi, soy sauce,
vinegar and sugar. Divide mayonnaise
mixture among bottom bun halves. Top
with tuna pieces and garnish with ginger
and coriander leaves. Cover with top
bun halves. Serve warm or at room
temperature.

THINK AHEAD
Cut buns up to 1 day in advance. Store in an airtight
container at room temperature. Assemble tuna
burgers up to 2 hours in advance.

COOKS' NOTE
Barbecue the tuna for the best flavour. Place tuna
on an oiled rack set 7.5cm (3in) above medium-hot
coals for 2 minutes on each side.

BASIC BOUCHEE RECIPE

MAKES 30
175g (6oz) puff pastry
1 egg yolk beaten with 1 tbsp water

ESSENTIAL EQUIPMENT
4.5cm (1¾in) fluted pastry cutter,
2.5cm (1in) fluted pastry cutter

Preheat oven to 200°C (400°F) Gas 6. Roll out pastry to a 3mm (⅛in) thickness. Stamp out 60 rounds with the larger pastry cutter. With the smaller pastry cutter, stamp out a circle from the centre of half of the pastry rounds (see below, left). This results in 30 pastry rounds and 30 pastry rings. Brush the pastry rounds with the beaten egg. Place pastry rings on pastry rounds (see below, right). Gently press to seal. Place topped rounds on a floured baking sheet. Brush again with beaten egg. Bake until risen and golden brown, 12 minutes. Cool on a wire rack. Cool to room temperature before filling.

THINK AHEAD
Bake up to 1 week in advance. Store in an airtight container in a single layer at room temperature.

TARRAGON AND MUSTARD LOBSTER BOUCHEES

MAKES 30
125g (4oz) cooked lobster meat, shredded
**1 tomato, peeled, seeded and diced
(see page 147)**
2 tbsp sliced tarragon
1 tsp creamy Dijon mustard
4 tbsp mayonnaise (see page 142)
salt, black pepper
1 recipe baked bouchées (see opposite)

Combine lobster, tomato, tarragon, mustard and mayonnaise. Add salt and pepper to taste. Use a teaspoon to fill bouchées with lobster mixture. Serve at room temperature.

THINK AHEAD
Make filling up to 1 day in advance. Cover and refrigerate. Fill bouchées up to 30 minutes before serving.

COOKS' NOTE
Chopped prawns or white crab meat are both delicious substitutes for the lobster in this recipe.

WILD MUSHROOM, GARLIC AND THYME BOUCHEES

MAKES 30
15g (½oz) butter
125g (4oz) wild mushrooms, finely chopped
1 shallot, finely chopped
1 garlic clove, finely chopped
1 tsp finely chopped thyme
2 tbsp crème fraîche
salt, black pepper
1 recipe baked bouchées (see opposite)
30 thyme sprigs to garnish

Melt butter in a frying pan over high heat. Add mushrooms, shallots, garlic and thyme. Stir-fry until tender and slightly crisp, 5–10 minutes. Stir in crème fraîche and remove from heat. Add salt and pepper to taste. Use a teaspoon to fill bouchées with mushroom mixture. Garnish with thyme. Serve hot or at room temperature.

THINK AHEAD
Make filling up to 1 day in advance. Cover and refrigerate. Warm through gently over a low heat with 1 tbsp extra crème fraîche. Fill bouchées up to 45 minutes in advance. Garnish just before serving.

WONTON CUPS

MAKES 20

150g (5oz) plain flour
125ml (4floz) boiling water

ESSENTIAL EQUIPMENT
2 - 12-cup mini muffin tins

Place the flour in a bowl and make a well in the centre. Pour in the water and mix with a fork to form a rough dough. Cover with a tea towel and let stand until cool enough to handle. Knead on a lightly floured surface until smooth and elastic, 5 minutes. Cover with a tea towel and let rest for 30 minutes.
Preheat oven to 200°C (400°F) Gas 6. Roll out dough on a lightly floured surface to a paper thin thickness. With a sharp knife, cut into about 20 squares, 5cm x 5cm (2in x 2in) each. Oil the muffin cups of both tins and line each one with a wonton pastry square. Bake until crisp, 10 minutes. Cool before removing from tins.

THINK AHEAD
Make up to 2 weeks in advance. Store in an airtight container at room temperature.

SQUID, SESAME AND LIME WONTON CUPS

MAKES 20

2 tsp sesame seeds
1 tbsp sesame oil
1 tbsp sunflower oil
grated zest of ½ lime
juice of 1 lime
1 tsp fish sauce
1 spring onion, finely chopped
150g (5oz) baby squid rings
1 recipe wonton cups (see opposite)

Toast seeds in a dry pan over low heat until nutty and golden, 3 minutes. Cool. Combine toasted seeds, oils, lime, fish sauce and spring onion; set aside. Bring a pan of water to the boil. Add the squid. When the water has returned to the boil, continue cooking for just 30 seconds. Drain and rinse under cold water. Pat drain on paper towels. Add squid to sesame lime dressing and stir to coat each ring well. Divide among wonton cups. Serve chilled or at room temperature.

THINK AHEAD
Make squid, sesame and lime salad up to 1 day in advance. Cover and refrigerate. Fill wonton cups up to 1 hour before serving.

FIVE-SPICE DUCK AND PAPAYA WONTON CUPS

MAKES 20

1 tsp runny honey
½ tsp five-spice powder
1 tsp dark soy sauce
1 duck breast, skinned
1 tsp rice wine vinegar
1 tsp sesame oil
1 tsp soy sauce
1 recipe wonton cups (see opposite)
½ papaya, diced
20 coriander leaves to garnish

Preheat oven to 200°C (400°F) Gas 6. Combine honey, spice powder and soy. Brush duck on both sides with honey soy mixture. Roast for 10 minutes. Cool completely. Cut across into very fine slices. Combine duck with vinegar, oils and soy sauce. Stir to coat each slice well. Divide duck among wonton cups. Top with papaya dice and garnish with coriander leaves.

THINK AHEAD
Cook and dress duck up to 1 day in advance. Cover and refrigerate. Dice papaya up to 1 day in advance. Cover and refrigerate. Fill wonton cups up to 1 hour in advance.

CUCUMBER CUPS WITH BLUE CHEESE MOUSSE AND CRISPY BACON

MAKES 20
6 streaky bacon rashers
125g (4oz) roquefort cheese
125g (4oz) cream cheese
salt, black pepper
1 spring onion, cut into strips
1 recipe cucumber cups (see opposite)
ESSENTIAL EQUIPMENT
piping bag with large star nozzle

Preheat oven to 180°C (350°F) Gas 4.
Place bacon rashers on foil-lined oven tray. Cook until golden and crisp, about 10–15 minutes. Drain on paper towels and cut into small triangular pieces. Beat cheeses until smoothly blended. Add salt and pepper to taste.
Fill piping bag with mousse (see page 146) and pipe into cucumber cups. Top with crispy bacon pieces. Garnish with spring onion strips.

THINK AHEAD
Prepare mousse up to 3 days in advance. Cover and refrigerate. Cook bacon up to 1 day in advance. Store in an airtight container in the refrigerator. Crisp in a preheated 180°C (350°F) Gas 4 oven for 2 minutes. Fill cups up to 1 hour before serving.

CUCUMBER CUPS

MAKES 20
1 cucumber
ESSENTIAL EQUIPMENT
3.5cm fluted pastry cutter, melon baller
Cut cucumber into about 20 - 1.5cm (¾in) thick slices. Stamp each slice with the pastry cutter (see opposite, left). Using melon baller, scoop out soft centres to make cups, leaving a 0.5cm (¼in) layer as a base (see opposite, right).

THINK AHEAD
Make cups up to 2 days in advance. Store in an airtight container in the refrigerator.

CUCUMBER CUPS WITH SMOKED TROUT MOUSSE, LEMON AND DILL

MAKES 20
150g (5oz) smoked trout
125g (4oz) cream cheese
½ tsp grated lemon zest
1 tbsp lemon juice
cayenne pepper
1 recipe cucumber cups (see above)
1 tsp paprika for dusting
20 dill sprigs to garnish
ESSENTIAL EQUIPMENT
piping bag with large star nozzle

Place smoked trout, cream cheese, zest and juice in a food processor or blender; pulse to a smooth paste. Add cayenne pepper to taste. Fill piping bag with mousse (see page 146) and pipe into cucumber cups. Dust with paprika and garnish with dill sprigs.

THINK AHEAD
Make mousse up to 1 day in advance. Cover and refrigerate. Fill cups up to 1 hour before serving.

CUCUMBER BARQUETTES WITH SMOKED SALMON AND PICKLED GINGER

MAKES 20
100g (3½oz) smoked salmon slices
20 pieces of pickled ginger
1 tsp wasabi
20 cucumber barquettes (see below)

Cut salmon into 20 - 0.5cm (¼in) wide strips. Put a piece of ginger on top of each salmon strip and roll up. Put a dab of wasabi on each cucumber boat. Top with a smoked salmon roll.

THINK AHEAD
Fill barquettes up to 1 hour before serving.

MAKING BARQUETTES
Peel and cut cucumber in half. Cut each half into 5cm length pieces. Use tip of knife to trim off 0.5cm (½ in) of flesh from the inside of each piece. Cut each piece into a diamond shape, about 5cm (2in) across.

CELERY BARQUETTES WITH STILTON AND WALNUTS

MAKES 20

8 large celery stalks
125g (4oz) stilton cheese
125g (4oz) cream cheese
salt, black pepper
1 tsp paprika to dust
20 walnut pieces to garnish

ESSENTIAL EQUIPMENT
piping bag with large star nozzle

Cut celery stalks on diagonal to make 20 - 5cm x 5cm (2in x 2in) diamond-shaped pieces. Beat stilton and cream cheese until well combined. Add salt and pepper to taste. Fill piping bag with cheese mixture (see page 146) and pipe into celery barquettes. Dust with paprika and garnish with walnuts.

THINK AHEAD
Make filling up to 2 days in advance. Cover and refrigerate. Prepare barquettes up to 2 days in advance. Store in an airtight container in the refrigerator. Fill barquettes up to 1 hour before serving.

CHERRY TOMATOES WITH CRAB AND TARRAGON MAYONNAISE

MAKES 20

20 cherry tomatoes
250g (8oz) white crab meat
4 tbsp mayonnaise (see page 142)
1 tsp creamy Dijon mustard
1 tbsp tarragon leaves, chopped
salt, black pepper

Cut and discard thin slices from stalk end of tomatoes to make flat, stable bases. Cut and reserve thin slices from smooth end to make tomato lids. Scoop out seeds with teaspoon and discard. Turn tomatoes upside down on paper towels to drain for 5 minutes. Combine crab, mayonnaise, mustard and tarragon. Add salt and pepper to taste. Use a teaspoon to fill tomatoes with crab mixture. Top with tomato lids.

THINK AHEAD
Prepare tomatoes up to 2 days in advance. Store in an airtight container in the refrigerator. Fill tomatoes up to 3 hours before serving. Cover and refrigerate.

RADISH CUPS WITH BLACK OLIVE TAPENADE

MAKES 20

150g (5oz) pitted black olives
4 anchovy fillets
2 tbsp capers
1 garlic clove, finely chopped
1 tsp lemon juice
1 tsp finely chopped thyme
2 tbsp olive oil
¼ tsp black pepper
20 round radishes

ESSENTIAL EQUIPMENT
melon baller

Place olives, anchovies, capers, garlic, lemon juice, thyme and oil in a food processor or blender; pulse to a thick paste. Add pepper. Cut and discard thin slices from radish bottoms to make flat, stable bases. Cut and reserve thin slices from radish tops to make radish lids. Using melon baller, remove most of radish centre to make "cups". Fill cups with tapenade. Top with reserved radish lids.

THINK AHEAD
Make filling up to 1 month in advance. Cover and refrigerate. Prepare cups up to 2 days in advance. Store in an airtight container in the refrigerator. Fill cups up to 1 hour before serving.

COOKS' NOTE
If you don't have radishes with tops, a sprig of dill will make a decorative and flavourful alternative garnish.

QUESADILLA TRIANGLES WITH HOT PEPPER RELISH

MAKES 24

6 - 15cm (6in) flour tortilla
1 tbsp sunflower oil
1 red pepper, quartered and seeded
2 green chillies, seeded and finely diced
½ garlic clove, crushed
1 tbsp olive oil
1 tbsp red wine vinegar

2 tbsp finely chopped coriander
¼ tsp granulated sugar
salt, black pepper
6 tbsp grated gruyère cheese
75ml (2½ floz) sour cream
1 spring onion to garnish

ESSENTIAL EQUIPMENT
cast-iron grill pan

Preheat grill pan over medium heat. Brush 1 side of a tortilla with oil. Place tortilla oiled side down on to the pan, pressing lightly with a spatula. Cook until just marked, 1 minute. Repeat with remaining tortillas.

For relish, grill and peel pepper quarters (see page 147). Finely chop grilled pepper. Combine pepper with chilli, garlic, oil, vinegar, coriander and sugar. Add salt and pepper to taste. Cover and let stand for 1 hour at room temperature to allow the flavours to blend. Preheat oven to 200°C (400°F) Gas 6. Place half the tortillas on a baking sheet. Sprinkle 1 tbsp cheese, then spread 1 tbsp relish over each tortilla. Sprinkle over another 1 tbsp cheese. Top with remaining tortilla. Bake until cheese melts, 5 minutes. Cool slightly.

For garnish, cut spring onion diagonally into 1cm (½ in) pieces. Cut each quesadilla into 8 wedges with kitchen scissors or a serrated knife. To garnish, top quesadilla triangles with sour cream and a piece of spring onion. Serve warm or at room temperature.

THINK AHEAD
Make salsa up to 1 day in advance. Cover and refrigerate. Prepare tortillas and fill up to 1 hour before serving. Cover and keep at room temperature.

COOKS' NOTE
We recommend wearing rubber gloves when working with chillies. Capsaicin, the substance in chillies that makes them hot and spicy, can cause a painful burning sensation if brought into contact with eyes or sensitive skin.

QUESADILLA TRIANGLES WITH SMOKY SHREDDED CHICKEN

MAKES 24

1 boneless, skinless chicken breast
3 tbsp sunflower oil
½ medium onion, finely chopped
2 garlic cloves, crushed
½ tsp ground cumin
½ tsp ground coriander
1 tinned chipotle pepper in adobo sauce (see page 162), chopped
1 - 200g (7oz) tin of chopped tomatoes

1 tsp tomato purée
½ tsp sugar
salt, black pepper
6 - 15cm (6in) flour tortillas
6 tbsp grated gruyère cheese
2 spring onions, finely chopped
75ml (2½ floz) sour cream
24 coriander leaves to garnish

ESSENTIAL EQUIPMENT
cast-iron grill pan

Place chicken in a pan with cold water to cover. Bring to a simmer over low heat. Simmer gently without boiling until cooked through, 7–10 minutes. Cool completely before draining. Drain and shred chicken.

Heat 2 tbsp oil in a skillet over medium heat. Stir-fry onion until softened, 5 minutes. Add garlic, cumin, coriander, chipotle, tomato, tomato purée and sugar. Cook until thickened, 5 minutes. Cool. Combine with shredded chicken. Add salt and pepper to taste. Preheat grill pan over medium heat. Brush 1 side of a tortilla with oil. Place oiled side down on to the pan, pressing lightly with a spatula. Cook until just marked, 1 minute. Repeat with remaining tortillas.

Preheat oven to 200°C (400°F) Gas 6. Place half the tortillas on a baking sheet marked side down. Combine cheese and spring onions. Sprinkle 1 tbsp cheese-onion mix, then 1 tbsp chicken over each tortilla. Sprinkle 1 tbsp cheese-onion mix over each topped tortilla. Top with remaining tortillas. Bake until cheese melts, 5 minutes. Cool slightly. Cut into 8 wedges with kitchen scissors or a serrated knife. Garnish triangles with sour cream and coriander leaves. Serve warm or at room temperature.

THINK AHEAD
Make chicken up to 1 day in advance. Cover and refrigerate. Prepare tortillas and fill up to 1 hour before serving. Cover and keep at room temperature.

MINI MUFFINS

MAKES 20

175g (6oz) plain flour
1 tsp baking powder
1 tsp baking soda
¼ tsp salt
6 tbsp caster sugar
1 egg, beaten
125ml (4floz) milk
3 tbsp melted butter

ESSENTIAL EQUIPMENT
2 - 12-cup mini muffin tins, buttered

Preheat oven to 200°C (400°F) Gas 6. Sift flour, baking powder, baking soda and salt into a bowl. Make a well in the centre. Add remaining ingredients, plus additional flavouring, if using. Gently fold everything together to make a wet batter. Spoon batter into 20 of the buttered muffin cups. Bake until golden brown and firm to the touch, 12 minutes. Turn out and cool completely on a wire rack.

THINK AHEAD
Bake muffins up to 1 day in advance. Store in an airtight container.

COOKS' NOTES
When flavoured, we think these mini muffins are delicious enough to be served without a filling. Place in a preheated 180°C (350°F) Gas 4 oven for 5 minutes before serving.

FLAVOURED MUFFIN VARIATIONS
ORANGE MUFFINS
Add grated zest of 1 orange to ingredients.

ROSEMARY MUFFINS
Add 2tsp finely chopped rosemary to ingredients.

ORANGE MUFFINS WITH SMOKED TURKEY AND CRANBERRY SAUCE

MAKES 20

1 recipe orange mini muffins
(see opposite)
4 tbsp cream cheese
150g (5oz) smoked turkey slices
4 tbsp cranberry sauce

Cut muffins in half. Spread each bottom half with cream cheese. Cut turkey slices into 20 - 2.5cm (1in) wide strips. Place 1 turkey strip on to each muffin. Spoon sauce on top. Cover with top half of muffin. Serve at room temperature.

THINK AHEAD
Fill muffins up to 3 hours before serving. Store at room temperature.

ROSEMARY MINI MUFFINS WITH SMOKED HAM AND PEACH RELISH

MAKES 20

1 recipe rosemary mini muffins
(see opposite)
1 peach, fresh or tinned
1 tsp cider vinegar
4 tbsp cream cheese
150g (5oz) smoked ham slices

For relish, cut peach into fine dice. Toss with vinegar. Cut muffins in half. Spread each bottom half with cream cheese. Cut ham slices into 20 - 2.5cm (1in) wide strips. Place 1 ham strip on to each muffin. Spoon peach relish on top. Cover with top half of muffin. Serve at room temperature.

THINK AHEAD
Fill muffins up to 3 hours before serving. Store at room temperature.

COOKS' NOTE
We highly recommend the combination of smoked duck and redcurrant jelly as an alternative filling for these flavourful rosemary mini muffins.

BABY BAGELS

MAKES 20

1 recipe unbaked bread dough
(see page 140)
1 egg yolk beaten with 1 tbsp water
2 tbsp poppy or sesame seeds

ESSENTIAL EQUIPMENT
Slotted spoon

Preheat oven to 200°C (400°F) Gas 6.
Divide dough into 20 walnut-sized
pieces. Shape each piece into a ball.
Form each ball into a ring by
inserting a floured finger into the
centre (see below). Work your finger
in a circle to stretch and widen the
hole. Bring a pan of water to the boil
over high heat, then reduce heat to
simmering. Working in batches, use
the slotted spoon to lower bagels into
the water. Boil until bagels rise to
surface, about 1 minute. Remove from
water to an oiled baking sheet with
the slotted spoon. Repeat with
remaining bagels. Brush bagels with
beaten egg and sprinkle with seeds.
Bake until golden, 10 minutes.

THINK AHEAD
Bake bagels up to 3 days in advance. Store in an
airtight container. Freeze bagels up to 1 month in
advance.

**FORM EACH
BALL INTO
A RING**
Insert floured
finger into the
centre. Work
finger in a circle
to widen the
hole.

BABY BAGELS WITH CREAM CHEESE, LOX AND DILL

MAKES 20

1 recipe baby bagels (see opposite)
125g (4oz) cream cheese
200g (7oz) smoked salmon
20 dill sprigs
black pepper

Slice bagels in half and toast lightly.
Spread bottom halves with cream
cheese. Top with salmon and dill and
sprinkle with pepper. Cover with top
halves. Serve at room temperature.

THINK AHEAD
Fill bagels up to 5 hours in advance. Cover and store
at room temperature.

BABY BAGELS WITH ROASTED RED ONION, GOAT'S CHEESE AND CHIVES

MAKES 20

2 red onions, roughly chopped
1 tbsp olive oil
salt, black pepper
1 recipe baby bagels (see opposite)
125g (4oz) fresh creamy goat's cheese
15g (½oz) chives, roughly chopped

Preheat oven to 200°C (400°F) Gas 6.
Toss onions with oil, salt and pepper.
Roast onions until soft, 15 minutes.
Slice bagels in half and toast lightly.
Spread each bottom half with goat's
cheese. Sprinkle with salt and pepper.
Top with red onions and chives. Cover
with top halves. Serve at room
temperature.

THINK AHEAD
Fill bagels up to 5 hours in advance. Cover and store
at room temperature.

CHOCOLATE CUPS WITH KIWI, RASPBERRY AND LIME MOUSSE

MAKES 20

125g (4oz) cream cheese
juice and grated zest of 2 limes
60g (2oz) caster sugar
125ml (4floz) whipping cream
20 bought mini chocolate cups
½ kiwi fruit, peeled
10 raspberries, halved

ESSENTIAL EQUIPMENT
piping bag with large star nozzle

Beat cream cheese with juice, zest and sugar until smooth. Whip cream until it holds soft peaks (see page 144). Fold cream into cream cheese mixture. Fill piping bag with mousse and pipe into chocolate cups (see page 146).
Cut kiwi across into 0.5cm (¼in) slices. Cut each slice into eighths. Garnish with kiwi triangles and raspberry halves.

THINK AHEAD
Fill cups up to 1 day in advance. Cover and refrigerate. Garnish up to 1 hour before serving.

CHOCOLATE CUPS WITH WHITE CHOCOLATE MOUSSE

MAKES 20

125ml (4floz) whipping cream
1 egg white
125g (4oz) white chocolate, melted
(see page 145)
20 bought mini chocolate cups
2 tbsp white chocolate flakes
1 tsp cocoa powder

Whip cream until it holds soft peaks (see page 144). Whisk egg white until it holds soft peaks. Fold melted chocolate into whisked whites, then fold in the whipped cream. Spoon mousse into chocolate cups. Refrigerate until set, about 1 hour. Garnish with white chocolate flakes and a dusting of cocoa.

THINK AHEAD
Fill cups up to 1 day in advance. Cover and refrigerate. Garnish up to 1 hour before serving.

COOKS' NOTE
To make chocolate flakes, grate white chocolate over the fine grate side of a cheese grater. To prevent the chocolate flakes from melting in your fingers, refrigerate the piece of chocolate briefly before you begin and hold the chocolate with a piece of grease proof paper as you grate. Use a teaspoon to sprinkle the flakes over each chocolate cup.

CHOCOLATE CUPS WITH MANGO AND MASCARPONE CREAM

MAKES 20

200g (7oz) tin of mango slices, drained
125g (4oz) mascarpone cheese
juice of ½ lime
1 tbsp caster sugar
20 bought mini chocolate cups
20 tiny mint sprigs to garnish

ESSENTIAL EQUIPMENT
piping bag with large star nozzle

Place mangoes, mascarpone, lime and sugar in a food processor or blender; pulse to a smooth purée. Fill piping bag with mango and mascarpone cream (see page 146). Pipe into chocolate cups. Garnish with mint sprigs.

THINK AHEAD
Fill cups up to 1 day in advance. Cover and refrigerate. Garnish up to 1 hour before serving.

CHOCOLATE CUPS WITH STRAWBERRIES AND ORANGE CREME FRAICHE

MAKES 20

150ml (5floz) crème fraîche
grated zest of 1 orange
20 bought mini chocolate cups
5 strawberries, sliced

Mix crème fraîche and orange zest together. Use a teaspoon to fill chocolate cups with orange crème fraîche. Garnish with strawberry slices.

THINK AHEAD
Fill cups up to 1 day in advance. Cover and refrigerate. Garnish up to 1 hour before serving.

SOBA NOODLES WITH SESAME GINGER VINAIGRETTE IN SPOONS

MAKES 20

250g (8oz) soba noodles
1 tbsp pickled ginger, finely chopped
2 tsp Chinese hot chilli sauce
4 tbsp rice wine vinegar
4 tbsp dark soy sauce
4 tbsp sesame oil
6 tbsp sunflower oil
2 tbsp sesame seeds

ESSENTIAL EQUIPMENT
20 Chinese or soup spoons

Bring a pan of water to the boil over medium heat and add the noodles. When the water returns to a boil, add 250 ml (8floz) of cold water. Continue cooking until water returns to a boil again. Repeat this process 1 or 2 times until the noodles are tender to the bite, 5–7 minutes. Drain and cool noodles in cold water. Let stand in the colander for 5 minutes to drain well.
Combine noodles, ginger, chilli sauce, vinegar, soy and oils and stir to coat the noodles well.
Toast seeds in a dry pan over low heat until nutty and golden, 3 minutes. Divide noodles into 20 equal-sized portions. Twirl each noodle portion around a fork to make a nest. Transfer to spoons. Garnish with sesame seeds. Serve at room temperature.

THINK AHEAD
Cook and dress noodles in vinaigrette up to 1 day in advance. Cover and refrigerate. Return to room temperature before serving.

COOKS' NOTE
Adding cold water to the noodles as they cook checks over-vigorous boiling to ensure that the noodles cook evenly.

FRAGRANT COCONUT SAFFRON PRAWNS IN SPOONS

MAKES 20

20 raw tiger prawns, peeled
1 lemon grass stalk
1 shallot, finely chopped
1cm (½in) piece fresh ginger, grated
1 garlic clove, finely chopped

pinch ground coriander
pinch saffron
1 tbsp sunflower oil
100ml (3½floz) coconut milk
¼ tsp salt, ¼ tsp black pepper

ESSENTIAL EQUIPMENT
20 Chinese or soup spoons

With a small sharp knife, cut each prawn almost in half lengthwise, leaving the tail end attached (see below, right).
Remove and discard the tough outer skin from the lemon grass and finely chop. In a non-metallic bowl, toss lemon grass, shallots, ginger, garlic, spices, oil and prawns together to coat each prawn well. Cover and refrigerate for 1 hour.
Remove prawns and place lemon grass mixture in a pan over a low heat. Cook gently, stirring, until fragrant, 5 minutes. Add coconut milk, salt and pepper. Bring slowly to the bowl over medium heat. Add prawns and simmer slowly until they turn pink and lose their transparency, 3 minutes. Arrange 1 prawn in each spoon. Drizzle over a little of the sauce just to coat. Serve warm.

COOKS' NOTE
For both of the recipes on this page choose spoons that sit well on a flat surface and are easy to pick up.

PASSION FRUIT CURD TARTLETS

MAKES 20

5 passion fruit, halved
juice of ½ lemon
4 tbsp sugar
60g (2oz) butter
1 egg, beaten
1 recipe baked pastry tartlets
(see pages 136–137)
2 tsp icing sugar for dusting

ESSENTIAL EQUIPMENT
small non-stick or heavy based saucepan

Scoop passion fruit pulp out of each half with a teaspoon. Combine passion fruit pulp, lemon and sugar in the saucepan. Add butter and place over a low heat. Stir occasionally, until the butter has melted. Place the egg in a bowl. Whisk egg constantly, while gradually pouring in the hot passion fruit mixture, until well blended. Return mixture to the pan. Cook over a low heat, stirring constantly, until thick and creamy, 10 minutes. Remove from the heat and continue stirring until cooled slightly. Cool completely. Divide curd among tartlets. Dust with icing sugar to garnish. Serve chilled or at room temperature.

THINK AHEAD
Make curd up to 3 days in advance. Cover and refrigerate. Fill tartlets up to 1 hour before serving.

COOKS' NOTE
Make lime or pink grapefruit curd for a refreshing alternative. Use 150ml (5floz) lime or pink grapefruit juice and 1 tsp grated lime or pink grapefruit zest instead of the passion fruit pulp and lemon juice.

CHERRY AND ALMOND FRANGIPANE TARTLETS

MAKES 20

30g (1oz) butter, softened
2 tbsp caster sugar
30g (1oz) ground almonds
1 egg yolk
1 tbsp double cream
1 recipe baked pastry tartlets
(see pages 136–137)
20 cherries (about 175g (6oz), stoned
2 tsp icing sugar for dusting

Preheat oven to 180°C (350°F) Gas 4. Combine butter, sugar, almonds, egg and cream until well blended. Divide evenly among tartlets. Place 1 cherry on top of each tartlet. Bake until set and golden, 15 minutes. Cool completely. Dust with icing sugar to garnish. Serve at room temperature.

THINK AHEAD
Bake filled tartlets up to 1 day in advance. Store in an airtight container at room temperature. Garnish just before serving.

COOKS' NOTE
Use tinned black or morello cherries when fresh cherries are out of season.

CITRUS GINGER CREAM TARTLETS

MAKES 20

grated zest and juice of 1 lime
grated zest and juice of 1 lemon
1 piece preserved stem ginger, chopped
5 tbsp double cream
175ml (6floz) sweetened condensed milk
1 recipe baked pastry tartlets
(see pages 136–137)
5 pieces of preserved stem ginger, sliced

ESSENTIAL EQUIPMENT
piping bag fitted with large star nozzle

Place lime and lemon zests, ginger, cream and condensed milk in a food processor or blender; pulse until combined. With the machine running, slowly pour in the lime and lemon juices until blended. Transfer to a bowl. Cover and refrigerate until set, 1 hour.
Fill piping bag and pipe filling into the tartlets (see page 146). Garnish with ginger slices. Serve chilled or at room temperature.

THINK AHEAD
Fill tartlets up to 1 day in advance. Cover and refrigerate. Garnish up to 2 hours before serving.

SUMMER BERRY TARTLETS

1 recipe vanilla pastry cream (see page 144)
1 recipe baked pastry tartlets (see pages 136–137)
200g (7oz) summer berries: raspberries, halved strawberries,
blackberries or blueberries
2 tsp icing sugar for dusting

ESSENTIAL EQUIPMENT
piping bag with large star nozzle

Fill piping bag with pastry cream (see page 146). Pipe into
tartlets. Arrange berries on top. Dust with icing sugar. Serve
at room temperature.

THINK AHEAD
Assemble tartlets up to 3 hours in advance. Keep at room temperature.
Dust just before serving.

BITTER CHOCOLATE TARTLETS

MAKES 20
75ml (2½floz) double cream
1 egg yolk
75g (2½oz) dark chocolate, broken into pieces
1 recipe baked pastry tartlets (see pages 136–137)
1 tbsp cocoa for dusting

Bring cream to a boil. Whisk boiling cream into the egg yolk
in a separate bowl. Add chocolate and stir until melted and
smooth. Allow to cool until slightly thickened, 30 minutes.
Spoon into pastry tartlets. Leave to set at room temperature.
Dust with cocoa. Serve chilled or at room temperature.

THINK AHEAD
Make filling and assemble tartlets up to 3 hours in advance. Cover and
refrigerate. Dust just before serving.

COOKS' NOTE
The chocolate flavour in this recipe is unadulterated, so use the brand of
chocolate you like best. More or less bitter depending on your preference.

CARAMELIZED LEMON TARTLETS

MAKES 20
1 egg, beaten
2 tbsp caster sugar
2 tbsp lemon juice, about 1 lemon
grated zest of 1 lemon
2 tbsp double cream
1 recipe baked pastry tartlets (see pages 136–137)
2 tbsp caster sugar to caramelize

Preheat oven to 190°C (375°F) Gas 5.
Whisk eggs and sugar together until sugar dissolves. Whisk in
lemon juice, zest and cream until just combined. Leave for 5
minutes. Skim any froth off the top. Pour lemon mixture into
baked tartlets. Bake until only just set, 5–8 minutes. Cool to
room temperature. Sprinkle tartlets with a thin layer of sugar.
Place tartlets under a preheated grill as close to the element as
possible until the sugar has coloured, 1–2 minutes. Watch
constantly to avoid burning. Serve at room temperature.

THINK AHEAD
Bake filled tartlets up to 1 day in advance. Cover and refrigerate. Caramelize
tops up to 3 hours before serving.

ORIENTAL CHICKEN WITH SPICY PESTO TARTLETS

MAKES 20

1 boneless, skinless chicken breast

2 tbsp light soy sauce

1 tbsp rice vinegar

1 tbsp sesame oil

1 tbsp sunflower oil

FOR PESTO

15g (½oz) coriander

10 mint leaves

1 green chilli, seeded

1 spring onion

1 tbsp roasted peanuts

1 tbsp sesame oil

1 recipe baked star-shaped sesame seed tartlets (see pages 136–137)

Place chicken in pan with cold water to cover. Bring to simmering over a low heat. Simmer gently without boiling until cooked through, 7 to 10 minutes. Cool completely in cooking liquid. Drain and shred chicken. Toss chicken with soy sauce, vinegar, sesame and sunflower oils. Place coriander, mint, chilli, spring onion, peanuts and oil in a food processor or blender; pulse to thick paste. Fill tartlets with chicken and top with pesto. Serve at room temperature.

THINK AHEAD

Cook chicken up to 2 days in advance. Cover and refrigerate. Prepare pesto up to 3 days in advance. Cover and refrigerate. Fill tartlets up to 2 hours before serving.

RARE ROAST BEEF WITH WHOLEGRAIN CREME FRAICHE IN POPPY SEED TARTLETS

MAKES 20

200g (7oz) rare roast beef slices

1 tbsp grainy mustard

6 tbsp crème fraîche

1 recipe baked star-shaped poppy seed tartlets (see pages 136–137)

20 tarragon sprigs to garnish

Cut beef slices into 2.5cm (1in) wide strips. Stir mustard into crème fraîche and divide among tartlets. Roll up beef slices and place on top of cream. Garnish with tarragon. Serve at room temperature.

THINK AHEAD

Make cream up to 1 day in advance. Fill tartlets up to 2 hours before serving.

PRAWNS WITH GINGER MAYONNAISE IN CORIANDER TARTLETS

MAKES 20

6 tbsp mayonnaise (see page 142)

1 tsp finely chopped ginger

½ tsp turmeric

200g (7oz) medium prawns, cooked and peeled

salt, cayenne pepper

1 fresh red chilli, seeded

1 recipe baked star-shaped coriander tartlets (see pages 136–137)

20 coriander leaves to garnish

Combine mayonnaise with ginger and turmeric. Add prawns, then salt and pepper to taste. Cut chilli into a very fine julienne strips (see page 147). Divide prawn mixture among tartlets. Garnish with chilli and coriander leaves. Serve at room temperature.

THINK AHEAD

Make filling up to 1 day in advance. Cover and refrigerate. Fill tartlets up to 2 hours before serving.

FETA, OLIVE AND ROSEMARY QUICHETTES

MAKES 20

60g (2oz) feta cheese, crumbled
1 egg yolk
3 tbsp double cream
black pepper
5 pitted black olives, quartered
20 rosemary sprigs to garnish
1 recipe baked pastry tartlets
(see pages 136–137)

Preheat oven to 180°C (350°F) Gas 4. Divide feta among tartlets. Beat egg and cream together. Add pepper to taste. Spoon egg mixture into tartlets. Top with olive quarters and rosemary sprigs. Bake until golden and set, 7 minutes. Serve warm.

THINK AHEAD
Bake up to 2 days in advance. Store in an airtight container in the refrigerator. Warm through in preheated 150°C (300°F) Gas 2 oven for 10 minutes.

BLUE CHEESE, MASCARPONE AND RED ONION CONFIT QUICHETTES

MAKES 20

1 recipe baked rosemary tartlets
(see pages 136–137)
30g (1oz) butter
1 medium red onion, finely sliced
¼ tsp salt
1 tbsp brown sugar
black pepper
60g (2oz) gorgonzola cheese, crumbled
3 tbsp mascarpone cheese
1 egg yolk

Preheat oven to 180°C (350°F) Gas 4. Melt butter in a frying pan. Stir in onions. Sprinkle with salt and sugar. Cook gently, stirring occasionally, until soft and dark, 30 minutes. Add salt and pepper to taste. Divide among baked tartlet cases. Crumble over blue cheese. Beat mascarpone and egg until combined. Spoon into tartlets. Bake until golden, 7 minutes. Serve warm.

THINK AHEAD
Bake up to 2 days in advance. Store in an airtight container in the refrigerator. Warm through in preheated 150°C (300°F) Gas 2 oven for 10 minutes.

FIELD MUSHROOM AND HOLLANDAISE TARTLETS

MAKES 20

30g (1oz) butter
1 shallot, finely chopped
200g (7oz) field mushrooms, chopped
1 tbsp cream cheese
2 tbsp lemon juice
salt, black pepper
1 recipe lemon hollandaise (see page 143)
1 recipe baked pastry tartlets
(see pages 136–137)
6 basil leaves, cut into chiffonade
(see below, right)

Preheat oven to 200°C (400°F) Gas 6. Heat butter in a skillet. Add shallots and mushrooms. Stir-fry over high heat until softened, 5 minutes. Cool slightly. Place mushroom mixture, cream cheese and lemon in a food processor or blender; pulse to a rough purée. Add salt and pepper to taste. Divide mushroom mixture among tartlets. Put 1 tsp hollandaise on top and heat through in the oven for 5 minutes. Sprinkle with basil. Serve warm.

THINK AHEAD
Make mushroom mixture up to 3 days in advance. Cover and refrigerate. Fill tartlets up to 2 hours before serving. Store at room temperature.

COOKS' NOTE
If you are short of time, use ready-made hollandaise, if you prefer.

MAKING BASIL CHIFFONADE
Stack basil leaves and roll them together tightly. Slice across roll to make very fine strips.

EGG, CAPER AND CRESS FINGER SANDWICHES

MAKES 30

4 medium eggs
1 tbsp finely chopped drained capers
15g (½oz) watercress, finely chopped
4 tbsp mayonnaise
salt, black pepper
45g (1½oz) butter, softened
10 medium slices white bread

Place the eggs in a pan of cold water. Bring water to a boil, then reduce heat and simmer for 8 minutes. Drain and cool eggs completely in cold water. Shell and chop eggs. Combine eggs, capers, watercress and mayonnaise. Add salt and pepper to taste. Spread butter, then egg mayonnaise evenly over 5 bread slices.
Top with remaining bread. Cut off crusts using a serrated knife and discard. Cut each sandwich in half, then cut each half into 3 fingers about 3.5cm (1½ in) wide. Serve chilled or at room temperature.

THINK AHEAD
Make sandwiches up to 1 day in advance, but do not remove crusts or cut. Cover with cling film and refrigerate. Cut sandwiches up to 3 hours in advance.

RARE ROAST BEEF AND HORSERADISH MAYONNAISE FINGER SANDWICHES

2 tbsp mayonnaise (see page 142)
2 tsp horseradish sauce
10 medium slices brown bread
150g (5oz) thinly sliced rare roast beef
45g (1½ oz) butter, softened

Combine mayonnaise and horseradish. Spread 5 bread slices evenly with horseradish-mayonnaise mixture. Top with roast beef. Spread butter evenly over remaining bread slices. Top beef with bread slices buttered-side down. Cut off crusts using a serrated knife and discard. Cut each sandwich in half, then cut each half into 3 fingers about 3.5cm (1½ in) wide. Serve chilled or at room temperature.

THINK AHEAD
Make sandwiches up to 1 day in advance, but do not remove crusts or cut. Cover and refrigerate. Cut sandwiches up to 3 hours in advance.

SMOKED SALMON AND CHIVE CREAM FINGER SANDWICHES

MAKES 30

175g (6oz) cream cheese
15g (½oz) chives, finely chopped
grated zest of ½ lemon
1 tbsp lemon juice
10 medium slices brown bread
200g (7oz) smoked salmon slices
black pepper
45g (1½oz) butter, softened

Combine cream cheese, chives, lemon juice and lemon zest. Spread mixture evenly over 5 bread slices. Top with smoked salmon and sprinkle with black pepper. Spread butter evenly over remaining bread slices. Top salmon with bread slices buttered-side down. Cut off crusts using a serrated knife and discard. Cut each sandwich in half, then cut each half into 3 fingers about 3.5cm (1½in) wide. Serve chilled or at room temperature.

THINK AHEAD
Make sandwiches up to 1 day in advance, but do not remove crusts or cut. Cover with cling film and refrigerate. Cut sandwiches up to 3 hours in advance.

AFTERNOON TEA CUCUMBER AND CHERVIL FINGER SANDWICHES

MAKES 30

½ cucumber, peeled and thinly sliced
½ tsp salt
90g (3oz) butter, softened
10 medium slices white bread
white pepper
2 tbsp finely chopped chervil

Place cucumber slices in a colander. Sprinkle evenly with salt. Cover and let stand for 1 hour. Pat cucumber dry with kitchen paper.
Spread butter evenly over all bread slices. Top 5 bread slices with cucumber. Sprinkle over white pepper and chervil. Top cucumber with remaining bread slices. Cut off crusts using a serrated knife and discard. Cut each sandwich in half, then cut each half into 3 fingers about 3.5cm (1½in) wide. Serve chilled or at room temperature.

THINK AHEAD
Make sandwiches up to 8 hours in advance, but do not remove crusts or cut. Cover and refrigerate. Cut sandwiches up to 3 hours in advance.

MINI CROQUE MONSIEUR

MAKES 20

10 medium white bread slices
5 ham slices
200g (7oz) gruyère cheese, grated

Preheat oven to 200°C (400°F) Gas 6. Top 5 bread slices with one slice ham each. Sprinkle half the cheese over the five slices. Press the remaining bread slices on top to make sandwiches. Place on a baking sheet. Sprinkle the remaining cheese across the top of the sandwiches. Bake until cheese is golden and melted, 10 minutes. Cool slightly. Cut off the crusts with a serrated knife. Cut each sandwich into 4 squares. Serve warm.

CROQUE MONSIEUR VARIATION

MINI CROQUE MADAME

Use 100g (3½oz) gruyère cheese instead of 200g (7oz). Fill sandwiches as directed but do not top with cheese. Bake until bread is toasted, 10 minutes. Cut sandwiches as directed. Fry 20 quail eggs in 30g (1oz) butter. Top each sandwich square with a quail egg. Sprinkle over salt and pepper and serve immediately.

THINK AHEAD
Assemble sandwiches up to 1 day in advance. Cover and refrigerate. Bake just before serving.

COOKS' NOTE
When making the croque madame, use the tip of a small sharp knife to crack open the quail eggs.

THE TECHNIQUES

A LITTLE EXTRA TIME AND EFFORT
FOR A SPECIAL OCCASION,
FOR FRIENDS, FOR FAMILY –
IT'S WORTH IT.

SHORTCRUST PASTRY

MAKES 300g (10oz)
175g (6oz) plain flour, sifted
¼ tsp salt
1½ tsp sugar
90g (3oz) chilled butter, cubed
1 egg yolk
2 tbsp water

Place flour, salt, sugar and butter in a bowl. Also add any flavouring, if using, to the bowl. With 2 knives, cut the butter into the dry ingredients until the mixture resembles fine crumbs (see opposite, left).

Add egg yolk. Mix with a wooden spoon to bring ingredients together. Add remaining water as necessary, ½ tbsp at a time, until the pastry begins to come together (see opposite, right). Bring the pastry together completely with your hands. Turn out of bowl on to a lightly floured surface. Knead briefly to make a smooth round.

THINK AHEAD
Make pastry up to 2 days in advance. Wrap in cling film and refrigerate. Return to room temperature before rolling out. Alternatively, make pastry and freeze up to 1 month in advance. Defrost overnight in refrigerator.

COOKS' NOTE
To ensure perfect pastry, have all the ingredients very cold. To guarantee the best results, place butter and flour in the freezer for 5 minutes before you begin.
As a general rule we do not recommend chilling the pastry, but if the weather is hot or the pastry has been over handled, wrap in cling film and refrigerate for 30 minutes before rolling out.

Cut in the butter with 2 knives.   Add the water ½ tbsp at a time.

FLAVOURED SHORTCRUST PASTRY VARIATIONS

Add the specified flavouring to the dry ingredients with the chilled butter. The flavouring ingredient will contribute extra moisture to the pastry, so you may need less liquid than usual to bind the pastry together.

CORIANDER PASTRY
Follow shortcrust pastry recipe, adding 1 tbsp finely chopped coriander to the dry ingredients.

POPPY SEED PASTRY
Follow shortcrust pastry recipe, adding 1 tsp poppy seeds to the dry ingredients.

ROSEMARY PASTRY
Follow shortcrust pastry recipe, adding 1 tsp finely chopped rosemary to the dry ingredients.

SESAME PASTRY
Follow shortcrust pastry recipe, adding 1 tsp sesame seeds to the dry ingredients.

USING A MACHINE

Follow recipe for shortcrust pastry. Place flour, salt, sugar and butter, with any flavouring, if using, in a food processor; pulse until mixture resembles fine crumbs. Add egg yolk; pulse until the pastry draws together. Add more water as necessary, ½ tbsp at a time. Turn pastry out of the machine on to a lightly floured surface and knead briefly by hand to make a smooth round.

BAKING PASTRY TARTLETS

MAKES 20
1 recipe unbaked shortcrust pastry

ESSENTIAL EQUIPMENT
20 - 4.5cm (1¾in) plain or fluted tartlet tins and 1 - 5cm (2in) plain or fluted pastry cutter

ALTERNATIVELY
2 – 12 cup mini muffin tins and 1 - 6.5cm (2½in) plain or fluted pastry cutter

Baking beans (bought ceramic beans, or alternatively, dried chickpeas)

Preheat oven to 200°C (400°F) Gas 6. On a lightly floured surface, roll out pastry to a 3mm (⅛in) thickness. Stamp out 20 rounds with the appropriate pastry cutter according to the type of tin specified by the recipe. Use the cut pastry rounds to line the tins (see below, left). Prick the base of each tartlet once with a fork. Refrigerate for 30 minutes before baking.

Fold a piece of baking parchment paper about 30cm (12in) long into small squares about 7cm (3in) x 7cm (3cm). Cut the folded paper along the folded ends with scissors. Separate paper to make about 21 paper squares. Do not discard paper liners after using, as they can be used again

Press a baking parchment paper square into each pastry case. Fill paper with baking beans (see below, right). Bake tartlets until firm, 10 minutes. Remove paper and beans. Continue baking until crisp and golden, 10 minutes.Cool slightly, then transfer to a wire rack.

THINK AHEAD
Line tartlet tins up to 1 day in advance. Cover and refrigerate. Bake tartlets up to 3 days in advance. Store in an airtight container at room temperature.

COOKS' NOTE
Roll out pastry between 2 large pieces of cling film to prevent pastry from cracking.
Lining the unbaked tartlets with paper and beans helps the pastry keep its shape when baked. If you are an experienced pastry maker and are confident that your pastry won't shrink, place the pastry tartlets in the freezer until solid and bake unlined from frozen.

Line the tartlet tins with the pastry rounds.

Bake tartlets filled with paper and beans to prevent pastry from shrinking in the oven.

MAKING STAR-SHAPED TARTLETS

Follow method for rolling out pastry given in the instructions above. Stamp out 20 rounds with a 8cm (3¼in) star-shaped pastry cutter. Butter 2 - 12-cup mini muffin tins and line each muffin cup with one star-shaped piece of pastry dough. Follow method for baking pastry (see above).

Stamp out the stars.

CHOUX PASTRY

MAKES 500g (1lb)

110g (3 ¾ oz) plain flour, sifted
175ml (6 floz) water
½ tsp salt
75g (1 ½ oz) butter
3 eggs

Place water, salt and butter in a pan over a medium heat. Bring just to the boil and remove from the heat. Add the flour to the pan, stirring constantly with a wooden spoon, until combined (see opposite). Return the pan to the heat and beat until the mixture is smooth and pulls away from the sides of the pan, 1 minute.

Remove from the heat and beat in the eggs, one at a time, making sure that each egg is thoroughly incorporated before adding the next one. Beat until the mixture is smooth, glossy and slightly sticky (see opposite).

USING A MACHINE

We recommend using a food processor only for making choux pastry in large quantities (ie; doubling or tripling the quantities given above). Make choux pastry as directed but transfer to a food processor before adding the eggs. While the machine is running, add eggs one at a time until the mixture is smooth, glossy and slightly sticky.

Add the flour and stir constantly with a wooden spoon until combined.

Remove from the heat and add the eggs one at a time.

CHOUX PUFFS

MAKES 35

1 recipe choux pastry (see page 138)

ESSENTIAL EQUIPMENT
2 tablespoons or a piping bag fitted with a large plain nozzle

Preheat oven to 180°C (350°F) Gas 4.

Use the tip of the 2 tablespoons to place small walnut-sized spoonfuls of choux pastry, 2cm (¾in) apart, on to a buttered baking sheet (see opposite). Bake until light, crisp and golden, 35 minutes. Cool on a wire rack.

Alternatively, fill the piping bag with the choux pastry (see page 146) and pipe small walnut-sized mounds, 2cm (¾in) apart, on to a buttered baking sheet. Bake until light, crisp and golden, 35 minutes. Cool on a wire rack.

THINK AHEAD
Bake choux puffs up to 3 days in advance. Store in an airtight container at room temperature. Alternatively, freeze baked choux puffs up to 1 month in advance. Defrost overnight in refrigerator. Crisp in a preheated 200°C (400°F) Gas 6 oven for 3 minutes.

COOKS' NOTE
Underbaked puffs do not keep, and turn soggy when filled. It is essential to check one puff for doneness before removing the entire baking sheet from the oven. Split open one puff: the interior must be hollow and completely dry. Continue baking if necessary until the puffs are completely dry.

Use the tip of 2 tablespoons to shape puffs.

Alternatively, use a piping bag.

CHOUX MINI ECLAIRS

MAKES 30

1 recipe choux pastry (see page 138)

ESSENTIAL EQUIPMENT
piping bag fitted with a large plain nozzle

Preheat oven to 180°C (350°F) Gas 4. Fill a piping bag with choux pastry (see page 146). Pipe out 30 spiral shaped strips about 5cm (2in) long on to a buttered baking sheet. Leave 4cm (1½in) between each strip to allow for expansion in the oven. Bake until light, crisp and golden, 35 minutes. Cool on a wire rack.

BREAD DOUGH

MAKES 400g (14oz)
250g (8oz) strong white flour
1 tsp salt
165ml (5½ floz) tepid water
1 tsp olive oil
1 tsp dried yeast

Place the flour in a bowl and make a well in the centre. Place the salt along the raised edge of the flour. Pour the water with the oil into the well. Sprinkle the yeast over the liquid. Leave for 5 minutes; stir to dissolve. Draw in the flour from the sides of the bowl with a spoon (see opposite, top), and mix to make a rough, sticky dough.

Turn out dough on to a lightly floured surface. Use the heel of your working hand to gently push the dough away from you. At the same time, use your other hand to rotate the dough slightly towards you, guiding it around in a circle (see opposite, middle). Repeat these kneading actions until the dough is smooth, shiny and elastic, 10 minutes.

Put the dough in a clean bowl and cover with a tea towel (see opposite, bottom). Leave to rise until doubled in size, about 1½ hours. Deflate the dough by pressing down with the palm of your hand. The dough is now ready to be shaped.

THINK AHEAD
Make and knead 12 hours in advance. Cover and leave to rise in refrigerator overnight. Let stand at room temperature for 30 minutes before shaping. Shape and bake according to the recipe.

COOKS' NOTE
The quantity of liquid required will often vary according to the type of flour used, as well as the level of humidity and temperature on the day of breadmaking. It is best to err on the side of making a dough too soft rather than too dry. Add extra water after drawing in the flour to form dough, as necessary, 1 tbsp at a time.

Draw in the flour from the sides of the bowl.

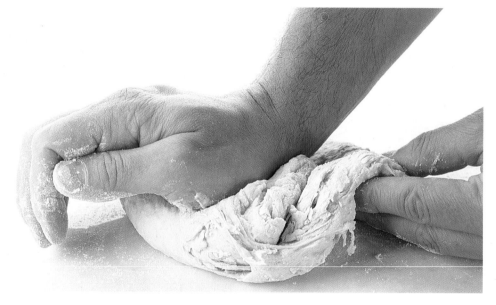

Knead the dough until smooth and elastic.

Cover the dough with a tea towel to rise.

USING A MACHINE
Follow recipe and method for bread dough, but place ingredients, after they have been mixed to a rough dough, into the bowl of a heavy-duty mixer fitted with a dough hook. To knead, set the mixer at low speed for 10 minutes.
Alternatively, use the bowl of a food processor fitted with a plastic dough blade. To knead, use the pulse button for 30 seconds at a time, until dough is smooth and elastic, 4 minutes.

VANILLA MERINGUE

MAKES 300ml (10floz)
2 egg whites at room temperature
125g (4oz) caster sugar
½ tsp vanilla extract

Put the egg whites in a large, clean bowl and whisk until the meringue holds soft peaks (see opposite).

Add the sugar, 1 tbsp at a time, whisking well after each addition (see opposite). Continue whisking until the whites are stiff and glossy. Fold in vanilla with a rubber spatula and any additional flavouring, if using, according to the instructions given for the flavour variations (see below).

COOKS' NOTE
Make sure the bowl is completely grease-free or your whites will not stiffen. If in doubt, wipe with kitchen paper dipped in vinegar before you begin.

A daring, but effective, way to check if the whites are sufficiently stiff is to hold the bowl upside down: the meringue should not fall out!

FLAVOURED MERINGUE VARIATIONS
Add the flavouring to the meringue with the vanilla. Fold in with a spatula until evenly combined.

CHOCOLATE MERINGUE
Fold in 1 tsp sifted cocoa powder with the vanilla.

HAZELNUT MERINGUE
Fold in 2 tbsp ground skinned hazelnuts with the vanilla.

MUSCAVADO MERINGUE
Fold in 1 tbsp dark brown sugar with the vanilla.

PISTACHIO MERINGUE
Fold in 1 tbsp chopped unsalted pistachios with the vanilla.

Whisk egg whites to soft peaks.   Add sugar 1 tbsp at a time.

VANILLA MERINGUE KISSES

MAKES 40
1 recipe unbaked vanilla meringue (see opposite, left)
ESSENTIAL EQUIPMENT
piping bag fitted with large star nozzle

Preheat oven to 120°C (250°F) Gas ½. Fill piping bag with meringue (see page 146). Pipe 40 meringue rosettes, 2.5cm (1in) apart, on to baking parchment-lined baking sheets. Bake until crisp and dry, 1 hour. Cool completely before removing from the baking sheet.

THINK AHEAD
Bake up to 1 week in advance. Store in an airtight container at room temperature.

Pipe kisses 2.5cm (1in) apart.

MINI MERINGUES

MAKES 20
1 recipe unbaked vanilla meringue (see opposite, left)

Preheat oven to 180°C (350°F) Gas 4. Use the tip of two teaspoons to place small walnut-sized spoonfuls of meringue, 2.5cm (1in) apart, on to baking parchment-lined baking sheets. Make an indent in the centre of each mini meringue with the back of one teaspoon. Bake for 5 minutes, then turn the oven temperature down to 120°C (250°F) Gas ½. Continue baking until firm to the touch, 20 minutes. Cool mini meringues completely before removing them from the baking sheet.

THINK AHEAD
Bake up to 2 days in advance.
Store in an airtight container at room temperature.

Shape meringue with the back of a teaspoon.

141

MAYONNAISE

MAKES 300ml (10floz)

2 egg yolks
1 tsp creamy Dijon mustard
1 tbsp red wine vinegar
½ tsp salt
pinch black pepper
1 tsp sugar
300ml (10floz) sunflower oil
black pepper

ESSENTIAL EQUIPMENT
wire whisk

Make sure that all the ingredients are at room temperature before you begin. Set a deep bowl on a cloth to prevent it from slipping as you whisk. Whisk the egg yolks, mustard, vinegar, salt, pepper and sugar together in a bowl until thick and creamy, 1 minute (see opposite, left).

Place the oil in a jug. Whisk in the oil a drop at a time until the mixture thickens. Add the remaining oil in a thin, steady stream, whisking constantly until thick and glossy (see opposite, right). Whisk in any flavouring, if using, according to the recipe variations. Adjust seasoning, adding more mustard, vinegar, salt, pepper or sugar to taste.

THINK AHEAD
Make mayonnaise up to 3 days in advance. Cover and refrigerate. Return to room temperature before stirring to prevent the mayonnaise from separating.

COOKS' NOTE
If the ingredients are too cold or the oil is added too quickly, the mayonnaise may separate. Don't throw it away! Combine 1 tsp vinegar and 1 tsp creamy Dijon mustard in a clean bowl. Whisk in the separated mayonnaise drop by drop until the mixture re-emulsifies.

SAFETY WARNING ON RAW EGGS
Because of the potential risk of salmonella, pregnant women, young children and anyone with a weakened immune system should avoid eating raw eggs. Make sure you use only the freshest (preferably organic) eggs, and if in doubt, substitute ready-made mayonnaise (see opposite).

Whisk the yolks until thick and creamy.

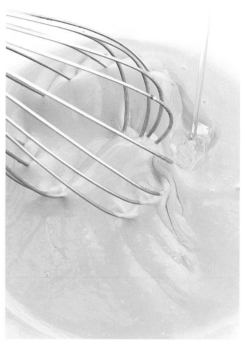

Add the oil in a steady stream.

FLAVOURED MAYONNAISE VARIATIONS
Whisk flavouring into the finished mayonnaise. Make sure that the flavouring and mayonnaise are at room temperature before you begin.

LEMON MAYONNAISE

Whisk 1 tbsp lemon juice into 1 recipe mayonnaise.

LEMON AIOLI

Crush 2 garlic cloves. Whisk crushed garlic into 1 recipe lemon mayonnaise (see variation above).

LIGHT LEMON MAYONNAISE

Whisk 2 tbsp warm water into 1 recipe lemon mayonnaise (see above) to lighten flavour, colour and consistency.

USING READY-MADE MAYONNAISE

Use ready-made mayonnaise when in need of a time saving short-cut or if health concerns are an issue for you. Seek out a good quality whole egg brand of mayonnaise and freshen the flavour by whisking in creamy Dijon mustard, sugar and red wine vinegar or lemon juice to taste.

USING A MACHINE

Follow recipe for mayonnaise. Place the egg yolks, mustard, vinegar, salt, pepper and sugar with 3 tbsp of the oil in a blender or food processor; process until blended, 10 seconds. While the machine is running, pour in the remaining oil in a thin, steady stream, until the mixture emulsifies and becomes thick and glossy. Pulse in any flavouring, if using. Adjust seasoning, adding more mustard, vinegar, salt, pepper or sugar to taste.

COOKS' NOTE
If using a food processor, depending on its capacity, you may need to stop the machine at intervals to scrape down the sides and over the base of the bowl with a spatula.

LEMON HOLLANDAISE

MAKES 175ml (6floz)

125g (4oz) butter
2 tbsp water
2 egg yolks
salt and white pepper
juice of ½ lemon

Melt the butter, then skim the froth from the surface with a spoon. Leave to cool until tepid. Place a heatproof bowl over a pan of simmering water set on a low heat. Make sure the base of the bowl is not in direct contact with the hot water. Place water and yolks with a pinch each salt and pepper in the bowl. Whisk the ingredients to a light and frothy mixture that holds the trail of the whisk, 3 minutes (see opposite, left). Remove the pan from the heat.

Whisk in butter, a little at a time, whisking vigorously after each addition, until the mixture emulsifies and becomes thick and creamy (see opposite, right). Gradually whisk in the lemon juice. Adjust seasoning, adding more salt, pepper or lemon juice to taste.

THINK AHEAD
Make hollandaise up to 30 minutes in advance. Keep warm in a bowl over a pan of hot water placed off the heat. Alternatively, make hollandaise up to 2 days in advance. Cover and refrigerate. Place in a heatproof bowl over a pan of simmering water set over a low heat. Make sure the base of the bowl is not in direct contact with the water. Warm through, whisking occasionally, until tepid, 10 minutes.

COOKS' NOTE
If the butter is added too quickly, the hollandaise may separate. Don't throw it away! Combine 1 tbsp water and 1 egg yolk in a clean bowl over a pan of simmering water set on a low heat. Make sure the base of the bowl is not in contact with the water. Whisk to a light and frothy mixture that holds that trail of the whisk, 3 minutes. Remove the pan from the heat. Whisk in the separated hollandaise, a little at a time, whisking vigorously after each addition, until the mixture re-emulsifies.

Whisk the water and egg yolks to a light, frothy mixture.

Add the butter a little at a time.

SAUCE BEARNAISE

Place 3 tbsp red wine vinegar, 6 peppercorns, 1 finely chopped shallot, and 1 sprig each tarragon and chervil in a small pan. Bring the ingredients to the boil over a medium heat and continue cooking until the liquid is reduced to 1 tbsp. Cool and strain. Now follow the recipe for hollandaise, omitting the lemon juice. Place the reduction in a bowl with the water, egg yolks, salt and pepper and follow the recipe method. Stir in 1 tsp each of finely chopped tarragon and chervil after the butter has been added. Adjust seasoning, adding more salt and pepper to taste.

USING A MACHINE

Follow recipe for lemon hollandaise. Place egg yolks, salt and pepper in a food processor or blender. Bring butter, water and lemon juice to simmering point in a small pan. While the machine is running, pour in the hot butter mixture in a slow, steady stream until the mixture emulsifies and becomes thick and creamy. Adjust seasoning, adding more salt, pepper or lemon juice to taste.

COOKS' NOTE
If using a food processor, depending on its capacity, you may need to stop the machine at intervals to scrape down the sides and over the base of the bowl with a spatula.

VANILLA PASTRY CREAM

MAKES 175ml (6floz)
2 eggs
2 tbsp sugar
2 tsp flour
125ml (4floz) milk
¼ tsp vanilla extract

Place the eggs and sugar in a bowl. Whisk until thick and light, 2 minutes. Add the flour and continue whisking until smooth (see opposite, top left).

In a small heavy-bottomed saucepan, bring the milk just to the boil over a medium heat. Pour the boiling milk into the egg mixture, while whisking constantly until the mixture is completely smooth (see opposite, top right). Pour the mixture through a sieve into a pan and place over a medium heat.

Cook the sieved pastry cream until very thick, stirring constantly, 2 minutes (see opposite, middle left). Reduce heat to low and cook, stirring constantly, until pastry cream no longer tastes of raw flour, 2 minutes. Stir in vanilla with any additional flavouring, if using, according to the recipe variation (see page 145).

Transfer pastry cream to a bowl to cool. Press greaseproof paper directly on to the surface of the pastry cream to stop a skin from forming (see opposite, middle right).

THINK AHEAD
Make pastry cream up to 2 days in advance. Cover and refrigerate.

COOKS' NOTE
Don't worry if lumps form as the pastry cream cooks; continue cooking. After removing from the heat simply push the cooked pastry cream through a sieve to eliminate any lumps. Be sure to allow the pastry cream to cool completely before chilling. If it is not completely cold when refrigerated, the steam will condense and form watery puddles on the surface of the cream.

Add the flour and whisk until smooth.

Whisk constantly while adding the milk to the egg.

Cook the pastry cream until very thick.

Cover with greaseproof paper to cool.

WHIPPING CREAM

For whipping, cream must contain a minimum of 30% butterfat.

Make sure the cream, bowl and whisk are well chilled before whipping: place in the refrigerator for 30 minutes or in the freezer for 10 minutes before you begin. Pour the cream into a bowl and whisk until it starts to thicken. Continue whisking until the cream is light and just holds a soft peak when the whisk is lifted. If the recipe requires stiff peaks, continue whisking until the cream stands up when the whisk is removed, about 1 minute more.

Whisk cream until it holds soft peaks. Add sugar and continue whisking until the cream re-stiffens to soft or stiff peaks, 1–2 minutes.

THINK AHEAD
Make whipped cream up to 4 hours in advance. Cover and refrigerate.

COOKS' NOTE
If your cream begins to look granular and yellowish as you are whisking you have over whipped it. To remedy, gently fold in a little extra cream, 1 tbsp at a time, to bring it back to a smooth, silky texture.

Whisk until cream holds soft peaks.

Add sugar to whipped cream and whisk to re-stiffen.

FLAVOURED PASTRY CREAM VARIATION

CHOCOLATE PASTRY CREAM

Follow the recipe and method for vanilla pastry cream. Melt 100g (3½oz) dark chocolate (see opposite). Stir melted chocolate into the pastry cream with the vanilla until thoroughly combined and smooth in texture.

MAKING CARAMEL

Place sugar and water in a heavy-bottomed pan over a low heat. Stir constantly with a wooden spoon. Do not allow the liquid to boil until the sugar has completely dissolved to a clear syrup. Raise the heat to medium and bring the syrup to the boil. Do not stir the syrup. Boil rapidly until the syrup starts to brown around the edge of the pan. Lower the heat and continue cooking, swirling the pan once or twice so that the caramel colours evenly. Remove the pan from the heat shortly before the caramel reaches the desired colour as it will continue to cook from the heat of the pan.

COOKS' NOTE

Once the syrup has boiled, do not stir as this encourages crystallization. If your caramel is colouring too fast, stop it cooking by plunging the base of the pan in to a bowl of cold water. If it sets too hard, warm it gently through in the pan over a low heat until it melts, taking care not to let it boil or to continue to cook further.

MELTING CHOCOLATE

Chocolate should be melted gently and slowly as it will scorch if overheated.

Break chocolate into small pieces. Place in a heatproof bowl over a pan of hot, but not simmering, water set over a very low heat. Make sure the base of the bowl is not in contact with the water. Once the chocolate starts to melt, stir frequently. When about half the chocolate has melted, remove the pan from the heat and stir constantly until smooth, glossy and completely melted.

COOKS' NOTE

Make sure the bowl fits snugly over the pan. If any steam escapes from the simmering water below and falls on to the chocolate as it melts, the chocolate may suddenly become rough, stiff and lumpy. If this should happen, remove the chocolate from the heat immediately and stir in sunflower oil, 1 tsp at a time, until the chocolate becomes smooth again.

Light caramel is pale gold in colour and is used for coating pastries.

Dark caramel is dark golden brown in colour and is used for lining moulds.

Once the chocolate begins to melt, remove from the heat and stir constantly until completely melted.

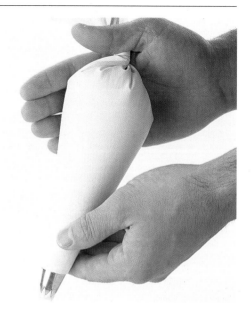

PREPARE THE PIPING BAG
Make sure the nozzle is fitted securely, then twist the bag above the nozzle to prevent leakage while filling.

FILL THE BAG
Fold the top of the bag over your hand to form a collar; spoon in the filling.

TWIST THE BAG TO PIPE
Twist the top of the bag, until the filling is visible in the nozzle, to clear any air pockets before you begin.

MAKING A PAPER PIPING BAG

Fold a 25cm (9½in) square of baking parchment in half diagonally and cut along the fold (see above). Bring one point of the triangle to the centre to form a cone (see top right).

Wrap the remaining point of the triangle around to meet the other two points. Pull all 3 points tightly together to create a sharp tip and fold flap inside (see bottom right). Crease the flap to hold the shape of the cone together.

PIPING, TOPPING OR FILLING

Hold the piping bag in a vertical position and exert pressure on the bag with the fingers and palm of one hand to force out the filling. Guide the nozzle with the other hand. Exert a small amount of pressure on the bag to make a small rosette for topping.

Apply additional pressure to make a large rosette for filling. Lift up the nozzle quickly to finish the rosette neatly.

CUTTING INTO JULIENNE STRIPS

Cut vegetable into very thin slices, about 0.3cm (⅛in) thick. Cut the stacked slices into thin even-sized strips the size of matchsticks. To save time, stack the slices a few at a time before cutting into strips.

PEELING TOMATOES

Cut a small cross, on the base of each tomato. Drop tomatoes into boiling water. Remove when you see the edges of the each cross begin to loosen, 10–20 seconds, depending on the ripeness. Drain, then immerse in cold water. Peel off the loosened skins, using the tip of a knife.

SEEDING TOMATOES

Cut tomatoes into quarters. With a sharp knife, cut out seeds and core.

Seeding tomatoes is crucial in many recipes because the seeds exude juice and may make fresh salsas and garnishes watery.

CUTTING INTO FINE DICE

Cut the vegetable into thin, even slices. Stack the slices a few at a time. Cut the stack lengthways to make equal-sized strips. Cut across to make an even-sized dice.

GRILLING AND PEELING PEPPERS

Roast pepper quarters skin side up under a hot grill until charred and wrinkled, 5–10 minutes. Place in a plastic bag or a bowl with a plate on top and leave until cool. The steam released by the peppers as they cool will loosen the skin.
Uncover cooled peppers. Peel off the charred skin, using the tip of a small knife. Scrape rather than rinse off any remaining bits of skin. Rinsing the pepper will wash away the roasted flavour.

PEELING CITRUS FRUIT

Cut a thick slice from both ends to expose the flesh. Stand upright and cut away peel and white pith, following the curve of the fruit.

SEGMENTING CITRUS FRUIT

Hold peeled fruit in one hand. Use the tip of the knife to cut down both sides of one white membrane to release each segment.

MAKING HERB SPRIGS

Select only the freshest, greenest leaves when making herbs sprigs for garnishing. Strip the leaves from the stalks and divide any larger sprigs into smaller pieces.

MAKING EDIBLE SKEWERS

Use edible skewers to add extra flavour to skewered foods. Some ideas used in the recipe section are illustrated here. Bay and thyme stalks are not shown, but also make effective skewers when their stems are stiff and thick enough to hold food.

LEMON GRASS SKEWERS

Remove and discard the tough outer skin from the lemon grass stalks. Cut in half lengthwise, keeping the stalks attached by the root. Cut into 10cm (4in) lengths to use for skewers.

ASSEMBLING A WRAP

ROLLING UP THE FILLING

Place the wrap base on a piece of cling film and cover with the filling. Use the cling film underneath to help you as you carefully roll up the base around the filling as tightly as possible.

SUGARCANE STICKS

If using fresh sugarcane, peel with a vegetable peeler and trim to 10cm (4in) lengths. Cut each sugarcane piece length-wise into 0.5cm (¼in) thick slices. Cut slices into 0.5cm (¼in) strips.

ROSEMARY SKEWERS

Strip the leaves from the stalks. Leave just a few leaves at one end. Sharpen the other end with a sharp knife to make threading food onto the skewer easier.

SECURING THE ROLL

Twist each end of cling film tightly to secure and shape the roll.

MAKING PARMESAN SHAVINGS

MAKING AN INDENT

Cut out a slightly curved indent from the longest side of the piece of chese with a sharp knife.

SHAVING THE PARMESAN

Use a vegetable peeler to shave curls from the indent

COVERING AIRTIGHT

Always press cling film against the surface of foods to keep out as much air as possible. The oxygen in the air increases the spoilage and discolouration of many foods, such as avocado. Protecting food from the oxidising properties of air will keep food looking and tasting fresher longer.

FREEZING UNBAKED ITEMS

To freeze unbaked items, spread out on a baking sheet and place in freezer uncovered until hard, 30 minutes. Once the items are frozen, pack into polythene freezer bags or an airtight container and return to the freezer. Remember to label items clearly for easier retrieval.

SEALING AIRTIGHT

Before sealing, expel all the air to make storage bags airtight. Zip lock polythene bags are ideal for storing both wet and dry foods. Zip lock bags are also useful for marinating. They allow the marinade to be evenly distributed around the ingredients.

HOT WEATHER COOKING

When planning a menu for hot weather, choose recipes that are fresh, light and simple to prepare. Not only do rich, creamy foods require cool temperatures for storage if made ahead, but they tend to be less popular in the warmer months. We advise starting as early in the day as possible, when the temperature is coolest. Do not attempt too many jobs at a time. Get one recipe finished and place immediately in a storage container in the refrigerator or in another cool place. Cool boxes with ice blocks are extremely useful in hot weather. They provide additional and portable refrigeration, especially when entertaining away from the house.

Take care to keep all food out of direct sunlight, both when storing and serving. For outdoor entertaining, find a shady, sheltered spot – and make sure it will still be in the shade during the hours you plan to entertain.

STORING IN LAYERS

Cooked pancakes and fritters and raw pastries and doughs are moist and may stick together if packed too tightly. Store in single layers in an airtight container with greaseproof paper or kitchen paper placed in between the layers to keep items separated.

THE PARTY

PLAN AHEAD,
CHOOSE A MENU WITH VARIETY,
PRESENT WITH SIMPLICITY AND STYLE;
YOU ARE SET FOR SUCCESS.

THE PLAN

THE MENU

The most crucial part of good menu composition is to include a variety of tastes, textures, aromas and colours. Try to create a menu with contrasts. Choose a variety of canapés that will give your guests a balance of sweet, sharp, spicy, salty and sour flavours. Remember that canapés should always be a small bite with a big flavour. Here are a few things to consider when planning your menu.

• Never attempt a menu with all brand new recipes. Experiment with unfamiliar recipes before the day of the party. Be sure to mix in a few tried and tested favourites.

• Let the seasons be your inspiration: seasonal ingredients will be reasonably priced, widely available and at their flavourful best. This will also help you avoid a time-wasting search for one ingredient.

• Review the guest list for vegetarians and anyone with special diet requirements, whether religious or medical.

• Provide something to please everybody. Be sure to consider both your more and your less adventurous guests. Include some old fashioned canapé classics as well as some creative new ones.

• Take into account how ingredients are prepared, whether grilled, fried, baked, roasted or raw, and try and achieve a good balance.

• Aim for a varied mix of ingredients and try not to repeat the same ingredient more than once in a menu.

• Include at least 2 hot canapés for parties during the colder months of the year.

THE QUANTITIES

A range of different factors play a part in how much your guests will eat. Canapé consumption goes up and down in direct relation to when, where and who.

TIME OF YEAR: we are heartier eaters in the colder months.

TIME OF DAY: consider when your guests will have last eaten a full meal. Guests who have had to travel or have arrived straight from the office to a party will eat more.

LOCATION: a crowded space makes serving difficult and as a result reduces the quantities consumed.

GUESTS: friends and family will not be afraid to tuck in at a casual gathering, whereas a formal occasion makes everyone more reserved and as a result they tend to eat less. At charity events, where the guests have paid for their invitation, value for the money will be an issue and as a result people will expect more food present.

The following quantities are only general guidelines, but can be a useful tool for menu planning.

Our basic rule is to allow 6 pieces per guest for the first hour and 4 pieces for each additional hour that the party continues.

For **pre-lunch or dinner drinks**, allow 3 pieces per guest and choose 3 different canapés.

For **canapés served instead of a first course before a lunch or dinner party**, allow 5 pieces per guest and choose 5 different canapés.

For a **2–3 hour drinks party**, allow 10 pieces per guest and choose 5 to 10 different canapés.

For a **canapés only party served in place of a meal**, allow 14 pieces per guest and choose either 7 or 14 different canapés.

For a **stand-up wedding reception,** allow 12 pieces per guest and choose 8–10 different savoury canapés and 2–4 different sweet canapés.

Focus on doing less better. We prefer to offer a smaller range of different kinds of canapés in a greater quantity. The finished product will be superior and you will save on time and cost. We recommend if you wish to serve 10 canapés per guest to choose 5 different recipes and double the quantities.

THE STRATEGY

Parties are to enjoy – and that goes for you as well as your guests. A party at home is more relaxed when you are well organised. Planning is everything.

• Make two shopping lists, one for dry goods and non-perishable ingredients that can be purchased in advance, another for foods that must be bought fresh the day before the party.

• Think through each recipe and make a cooking timetable. List all the stages of preparation, from complete recipes suitable for freezing to any last minute garnishing that needs to be done just before serving.

• Prepare ingredients and cook ahead as much as possible so you have plenty of time to complete the final preparations without suffering from party day panic. Use the THINK AHEAD advice provided for each recipe in the book.

• Enlist family and friends, or hire professionals, to help you serve.

• Take stock of your serving dishes before the day of the party. Make sure you have enough and make arrangements to buy, borrow or hire if necessary.

THE PRESENTATION

GENERAL RULES

Canapés must be tempting to the eye as well as pleasing to the palate. If food looks fabulous, people will feel confident that it tastes fabulous too. Follow these tips for beautiful, mouthwatering results.

• Arrange one, or at most two, kinds of canapés on a serving tray at a time. Too many kinds is not only visually confusing, but unpractical, as guests have to break the flow of conversation to make their choice.

• Place canapés in neat, evenly spaced rows to maximise their aesthetic appeal.

• Odd numbers look better than even numbers, and diagonal lines are more pleasing to the eye than straight ones. Remember this golden rule of food presentation when arranging canapés on a serving tray.

• Don't overcrowd the serving trays. A densely packed arrangement can look cluttered and messy rather than generous.

• Keep garnishes simple. Over decorated food can look fussy and unappetising.

• Make sure your guests have somewhere to put skewers or shells after they have finished eating a canapé.

• Avoid plates and platters that will be heavy or difficult to pass.

• Get help assembling canapés and arranging garnishes and trays. These final preparations are great fun when shared with family and friends.

• Have more napkins on hand than you think you'll need. When offering food, always have cocktail napkins handy for any guests who might need one.

NATURAL CONTAINERS AND GARNISHES

Fresh, edible garnishes are a simple, natural way to decorate (see pages 156–157).

Use brightly coloured fruits and vegetables to garnish platters and trays. Hollow them out to make edible containers for nibbles, dippers and dips. A serrated knife and a melon baller (see page 14) are essential tools for this. Prepare edible decorations up to 1 day in advance and store covered with damp kitchen paper in an airtight container in the refrigerator.

CREATIVE SERVING IDEAS

Innovative presentation need not cost the earth and always makes food memorable and for some, even more delicious (see pages 158–159).

Fresh herbs make natural sticks for skewering (see page 148), fragrant bouquets for garnishing and an aromatic lining for a serving tray. Choose herbs unlikely to wilt, like rosemary, thyme, oregano, bay, lemon grass and sage.

Use leaves to line trays or platters. Be sure to wipe fresh leaves clean with a damp cloth. Banana, rhubarb, fig, vine, palm and cabbages leaves of all colours are ideal. Dried leaves, such as chestnut or lotus, should be brushed with sunflower oil before using.

Visit Asian and other ethnic stores for unusual but inexpensive serving ideas. A bamboo steamer used as a serving dish, chopsticks as skewers, sushi mats and noodles to line trays: these are all easy and inexpensive ways to add style to the presentation of an oriental-themed canapé menu. Use your imagination to come up with ideas of your own.

STATIONARY CANAPES

Canapé parties are an easy way to entertain a large number of people at home. Think, no chairs, no plates, no cutlery!
If you are expecting more than 15 guests, you will need helping hands, be they hired professionals or recruits from family and friends. But not all the food has to be handed round. A less formal approach is to arrange everything on stationary platters and trays, in bowls and baskets. Place on tables around the room and allow people to serve themselves.

Natural Containers and Garnishes

1. MINIATURE PINEAPPLES: Use whole to decorate a stationary arrangement of canapés.

2. NAVEL ORANGE: Julienne peel to garnish sweet or savoury canapés.

3. SWEET RED PEPPER: Hollow out to hold dips and sauces.

4. SMALL AUBERGINE: Use whole to decorate a serving tray.

5. BUTTERNUT SQUASH: Hollow out to hold vegetable dippers.

6. ITALIAN PEPPER: Use whole to decorate a serving tray of spicy canapés.

7. STAR FRUIT: Slice to garnish a serving tray of sweet canapés.

8. CHARENTAIS MELON: Hollow out to hold fruit skewers and dipping sauces.

9. PURPLE AND WHITE CABBAGE: Hollow out to use as a container for dips.

10. LIMES AND LEMONS: Peel and segment to garnish individual canapés.

CREATIVE SERVING IDEAS

1. WICKER BASKET: To serve stacked canapés (see page 132).
2. SUSHI MAT: To line a serving tray (see page 90).
3. BANANA LEAVES: To line a serving tray (see page 73).
4. COARSE SEA SALT: To support shellfish canapés (see page 104).
5. BAMBOO STEAMER: To serve Asian-style canapés.
6. CHOP STICKS: As an alternative to wooden skewers (see page 71).
7. SOBA NOODLES: To line a serving tray (see page 94).
8. LEMON GRASS STALKS: To skewer grilled chicken (see page 74).
9. WOODEN TOOTHPICKS: To skewer bite-sized canapés (see page 68).
10. WOODEN SKEWERS
11. WOVEN TABLE MAT
12. SLATTED WOODEN TRAY
13. ROSEMARY SPRIG SKEWERS (see page 71).

MENU SUGGESTIONS
(see the index for page numbers)

DO NOTHING ON THE DAY

Consult this list for canapés that keep you out of the kitchen on the day of the party. All can be made at least 1 day ahead and transferred from storage container to serving tray with minimal effort.

Parmesan and Anchovy Palmiers

Cherry and Almond Frangipane Tartlets

Chorizo Puffs

Citrus Ginger Cream Tartlets

Creamy Blue Cheese and Spring Onion Dip

Crispy Potato Skins

Crunchy Sweet and Spicy Pecans

Curry Puffs

Curry Spiced Yoghurt, Coriander and Mango Chutney Dip

Ham and Dijon Mini Croissants

Egg, Caper and Cress Finger Sandwiches

Herbed Yoghurt Dip

Herbed Pita Crisps

Honey Mustard and Prosciutto Palmiers

Mediterranean Marinated Olives

Mini Gougères

Queen Olive Cheese Balls

Oven-Dried Root and Fruit Chips

Rare Roast Beef and Horseradish Mayonnaise Finger Sandwiches

Roast Red Pepper, Feta and Mint Dip

Rolled Smoked Ham Crepes with Tarragon and Mustard Cream

Rolled Ricotta and Sage Crepes with Parmesan Shavings

Salsa Romesco Dip

Savoury Sables

Smoked Salmon and Chive Cream Finger Sandwiches

Smoked Salmon Ruggelash

Smoked Salmon Sushi Rice Balls

Spicy Peanut Dip

Spinach, Smoked Trout and Herbed Cream Roulades

Spiced Party Nuts

Spiced Roast Aubergine Dip

Sun-dried Tomato and Cannellini Bean Dip

Sun-dried Tomato Pesto Palmiers

Swiss Cheese Allumettes

Texas Red Bean Wraps with Coriander Crema

Vegetable Dippers

•

CANAPES FROM THE GRILL

Let your guests mingle over some tasty nibbles while the barbecue heats up. Follow with food hot off the grill. Finish with a decadent dessert.

Crunchy Sweet and Spicy Pecans

Herbed Yoghurt Dip with Crispy Potato Skins

Clams with Ginger and Lime Butter

Ginger Hoisin Chicken Drummettes

Lemon Chilli Prawn Sticks

Curried Coconut Chicken Sticks

Quesadilla Triangles with Hot Pepper Relish

Strawberry and Pistachio Mini Meringues

•

LIGHT BITES FOR AL FRESCO ENTERTAINING

A midsummer menu for a lively party under the hot midday sun – serve in place of a first course, or double up the quantities and make it a meal.

Chilled Spiced Chickpea Soup with Avocado Salsa

Tomato and Basil Crostini

Basil Marinated Mozzarella and Cherry Tomato Skewers

Radish Cups with Black Olive Tapenade

Mini Peking Duck Pancakes with Plum Sauce

CELEBRATION BRUNCH FOR THE FAMILY

Classic canapés for a brunch party appeal to young and old alike. Perfect with your favourite fruit juice and fizz, everything but the croque monsieur can be prepared a day ahead and assembled well in advance.

Ham and Dijon Mini Croissants

Egg and Bacon Puffs

Mini Croque Monsieur

Baby Bagels with Cream Cheese, Lox and Dill

Rosemary Mini Muffins with Smoked Ham and Peach Relish

Tiny Dill Scones with Smoked Trout and Horseradish Cream

Tropical Fruit Brochettes with Passion Fruit and Mascarpone Dip

•

ELEGANT APPETIZERS FOR A SHORT FORMAL RECEPTION

Prelude to an elegant evening of entertaining – many of these can be started ahead, but you will need an extra pair of hands just before serving to help with the final touches.

Chive-Tied Crepe Bundles with Smoked Salmon and Lemon Creme Fraiche

Tarragon and Mustard Lobster Bouchees

Baby Baked Potatoes with Sour Cream and Caviar

Asparagus Croutes with Lemon Hollandaise

Carpaccio Canapés

•

FAST AND FABULOUS MENU

Good food in a hurry – use the THINK AHEAD notes to get the dip and crostini finished before guests arrive. Grill the chicken and prawn sticks to order. You've done it.

Creamy Blue Cheese and Spring Onion Dip with Herbed Pita Crisps

Avocado and Goat's Cheese Crostini

Curried Coconut Chicken Sticks

Tangy Thai Prawn Skewers

PORTABLE CANAPES FOR AN EVENING IN THE PARK

A varied menu that can be completely prepared in advance and transported easily – bring along wicker baskets, wooden bowls and large napkins and arrange the food once you arrive at the perfect spot.

Swiss Cheese Allumettes

Salsa Romesco Dip with
    Vegetable Dippers

Mini Pissaladiere

Spicy Pork Empanaditas with Chunky
    Avocado Relish

Roast Red Onion and Thyme
    Foccacine

Minted Feta and Pine Nut Filo Rolls
    with Lemon Aioli

Triple Chocolate Biscottini with
    Hazelnuts

CANDELIGHT WINTER WEDDING AT HOME

A welcoming, warming menu of traditional canapés with a twist – we recommend starting the preparation two days in advance; refer to the THINK AHEAD *notes.*

Carrot, Honey and Ginger Soup Cups

Cocktail Salmon and Dill Cakes with
    Crème Fraîche Tartare

Field Mushroom and
    Hollandaise Tartlets

Orange Muffins with Smoked Turkey
    and Cranberry Sauce

Filo Tartlets with Smoked Salmon,
    Cracked Pepper and Lime

Quail Egg, Caviar and Chervil
    Croustades

Grilled Beef Fillet with Salsa
    Verde Croutes

Chive Pancakes with Crème Fraîche
    and Red Onion Confit

Cherubs on Horseback

Mini Mango Galettes

Bitter Chocolate Tartlets

Mini Sticky Orange and
    Almond Cakes

MEDITERRANEAN FEAST

A big on flavour, make ahead menu for a special occasion.

Parmesan and Pine Nut Biscottini
    with Green Olives

Sundried Tomato and Cannellini Bean
    Dip with Herbed Pita Crisps

Spicy Prawn Crostini

Artichoke and Gorgonzola Focaccine

Feta, Olive and Rosemary Quichettes

Polenta Crostini with Tomato and
    Black Olive Salsa

Chicken, Prosciutto and Sage Spiedini
    with Roast Pepper Aioli

TEMPTING TREATS FOR AN INFORMAL EVENING WITH FRIENDS

Simple and delicious food to relax with and enjoy – everything can be made well ahead of your guests arrival. The skewers are the only item that require last minute attention.

Mediterranean Marinated Olives

Savoury Sables

Roast Red Pepper, Feta and Mint
    Dip with Vegetable Dippers

Filo Tartlets with Spicy
    Coriander Prawns

Wild Rice and Spring Onion Pancakes
    with Avocado Lime Salsa

Sesame Soy Glazed Beef Skewers

Mini Chocolate Truffle Cake

VEGETARIAN CANAPES FOR A CROWD

Fabulous finger food without meat or fish – combine a range of vegetables with fragrant herbs, pungent cheeses and crisp pastries to tempt even the most hardened of carnivores.

Queen Olive Cheese Balls

Twisted Parsley Breadsticks

Lemon Marinated Tortellini and
    Sun-dried Tomato Skewers

Mini Cherry Tomato and Basil
    Pesto Galettes

Roast Pepper, Goat's Cheese and
    Mint Wraps

Crispy Carrot and Spring Onion
    Cakes with Feta and Black Olive

Herbed Artichoke and Parmesan
    Filo Rolls with Light Lemon
    Mayonnaise Dip

Focaccine Farcite with Wild
    Mushrooms and Thyme

Aubergine and Pine Nut Fritters with
    Roast Tomato Sauce

Polenta Crostini with Blue Cheese and
    Balsamic Red Onions

AFTERNOON TEA MENU FOR A SUMMER WEDDING

A mix of teatime classics and contemporary inspirations – this menu sets the scene for a truly memorable occasion. Read through the THINK AHEAD *notes and begin preparation two days in advance.*

Smoked Salmon and Chive Cream
    Finger Sandwiches

Egg, Caper and Cress Finger
    Sandwiches

Gingered Chicken Cakes with
    Coriander Lime Mayonnaise

Tiny Parmesan and Rosemary
    Shortbreads with Roast Cherry
    Tomatoes and Feta

Valentine Cucumber Cream Canapés

Dill Pancakes with Salmon Caviar and
    Lemon Creme Fraiche

Rare Roast Beef with Wholegrain
    Mustard in Poppy Seed Tartlets

Mangetout Wrapped Prawn Skewers
    with Lemon Mayonnaise

Filo Tartlets with Bang Bang Chicken

Cucumber Cups with Smoked Trout
    Mousse, Lemon and Dill

Tiny Shortcakes with
    Strawberries and Cream

Mini Raspberry Ripple
    Meringue Kisses

NOTES FROM THE COOKS ON THE INGREDIENTS

ANCHOVY FILLETS If you find the flavour of anchovies too pungent, soak them in milk for 10 minutes before using.

ARTICHOKE We use jars of baby globe artichoke hearts marinated in oil. They are also available tinned in brine. These tend to be slightly larger, so you may need to cut them accordingly.

AUBERGINE A **medium aubergine** weighs about 300g (10oz).

AVOCADO A **small avocado** weighs about 175g (6oz); a **medium avocado** weighs about 250g (8oz); a **large avocado** weighs about 350g (12oz).

BEETROOT A small beetroot weighs about 125g (4oz).To cook raw beetroot, bake unpeeled in a preheated 150°C (300°F) Gas 2 oven until tender, 1 hour.

BREADCRUMBS To make **fresh breadcrumbs**, cut bread into slices, cut off crusts and cut into pieces. Place in a blender or food processor; pulse until finely ground. Store in an airtight container for up to 2 days.
To make **dried breadcrumbs**, cut day-old bread into slices, cut off the crusts. Bake in a preheated 150°C (300°F) Gas 2 oven until dry and crisp, 10 minutes. Place in a blender or food processor; pulse until finely ground. Store in an airtight container for up to 1 month.

BUCKWHEAT FLOUR Grey-brown in colour with a distinct bitter flavour; available at healthfood stores and in large supermarkets.

BUTTER For us means unsalted or lightly salted butter.

CAPERS The pickled bud of the caper plant. We use regular and baby ones (see page 13); always drain well before using.

CARDAMOM Best used freshly ground as its fragrance diminishes with time. Open, discard the seed pods and crush the black or brown seeds.

CAVIAR (see page 10). Salted fish roe (eggs) available in various qualities and at hugely varying prices. A little goes a long way.

CHEESE Fresh **creamy goat's cheese** is a fresh, white, rindless, lightly sour cheese, available in rolls, rounds or pyramids. As an alternative, combine 3 parts cream cheese with 1 part Greek-style yoghurt until smooth.
Dolcelatte cheese is a creamy, blue veined Italian cheese with a mild flavour. Use a mild blue cheese as an alternative.
Gorgonzola cheese is a rich, blueish green veined Italian cheese with a piquant flavour. Use a strong blue cheese as an alternative.
Gruyère cheese is a hard Swiss cheese with a sweet, nutty flavour. Unlike so many hard cheeses, it melts without becoming oily or rubbery. Use Emmenthal or a hard yellow cheese as an alternative.
Mascarpone cheese is a rich, velvety Italian cream cheese. As an alternative, mix 3 parts cream cheese with 1 part double cream and a pinch of sugar until smooth.
Parmesan cheese (see page 10) is an Italian hard cheese with a rich, sharp flavour that is nothing like the smelly, cheesy taste of ready-grated parmesan that is sold in a tub. Always buy parmesan by the piece and grate as required.
Roquefort cheese (see page 10) is a rich, creamy, green-veined French cheese made from ewe's milk with a piquant flavour. Use a strong blue cheese as an alternative.
Stilton cheese (see page 10) is a rich, crumbly blueish green veined British cheese with a pungent flavour. Use a strong blue cheese as an alternative.

CHERVIL A very delicately flavoured herb; use flat-leaf parsley as an alternative.

CHILLI There are over 200 different varieties of fresh chillies, varying in colour, size, shape and heat. As a general rule, the smaller the chilli the hotter it is. Capsaicin, the substance in chillies is responsible for their heat, and can cause a very painful burning sensation if it comes into contact with the eyes, the mouth or other sensitive skin. Make sure you wash your hands thoroughly after handling chillies, or wear rubber gloves. To reduce the level of heat remove the seeds before using.
Crushed chillies (see page 12) are a widely available hot seasoning or can be made at home by crushing dried chillies in a pestle and mortar or an electric grinder. **Chipotles in Adobo** (see page 13) are dried smoked jalapeno chillies pickled and tinned in a piquant sauce made from chillies, herbs and vinegar. Available mail order or from speciality stores.

CHILLI SAUCE We use two different types; **Chinese hot chilli sauce** (see page 12), made from chillies, salt and vinegar, and **Thai sweet chilli sauce** (see page 12), flavoured with ginger and garlic as well as sugar, salt, vinegar and chillies. Both available in large supermarkets or in Asian stores.

CHINESE PANCAKES Available chilled and frozen in Asian stores and large supermarkets.

CHIPOTLES IN ADOBO (see chillies).

CHORIZO Pork sausage flavoured and coloured with paprika much used in Spanish and Mexican cooking. It can be mild or highly spiced. It is mostly available cured when it can be eaten without cooking.

CREME FRAICHE Thick cream with a slightly sour flavour and a velvety texture. It keeps longer than ordinary cream and can be boiled without curdling. For cooking, substitute double cream. For garnishing, substitute equal parts of whipped double cream (see page 144) combined with Greek-style yoghurt.

COCONUT MILK We used tinned, which is available at Asian stores and large supermarkets. Shake well before opening.

CORN Available fresh on the cob or as frozen or tinned kernels. To cut kernels from the cob, stand the corn upright and carefully cut downwards with a sharp knife.

CORN MEAL We use yellow, medium-ground cornmeal; use Italian polenta as an alternative.

CORNICHONS Crisp pickles made from tiny gherkin cucumbers; also called cocktail gherkins.

CRAB When buying cooked crab in the shell, choose one that feels heavy for its size. Whether bought fresh, tinned or frozen, cooked crabmeat should be picked over with your fingers to remove any membrane or shell.

DUMPLING WRAPPERS Small rounds of fresh noodle dough available fresh and frozen in Chinese stores or good supermarkets. They can be stored in the refrigerator for up to 1 week if well wrapped.

EGGS We use large; in practice this means 1 beaten egg is 3 tbsp beaten egg, 1 egg yolk is 1 tbsp egg yolk, and 1 egg white is 2 tbsp egg white. **Quail eggs** (see page 11) are available at Chinese stores and in the gourmet section of large supermarkets. They are difficult to peel, so plunge them into cold water as soon as they are cooked and peel them at once under cold running water. Refrigerate peeled in water.

FIGS Best in the late summer and early autumn months.

FISH SAUCE Thin, salty brown sauce made from fermented fish used extensively in Southeast Asian cooking. Available in large supermarkets and Asian stores. We use **Thai fish sauce** called nam pla; use light soy sauce as an alternative.

FIVE SPICE POWDER Chinese spice blend of ground cloves, cinnamon, fennel, star anise and szechuwan peppercorns.

FRUIT in all of the recipes should be washed and, unless otherwise stated, peeled.

GARLIC Unless we indicate otherwise, all garlic cloves are medium-sized.

GINGER Do not substitute ground ginger for **fresh ginger**, the flavours are quite different. Store fresh ginger wrapped in the refrigerator for up to 3 weeks. Cut off the skin with a sharp knife before measuring. **Preserved stem ginger** is fresh ginger preserved in jars in a thick syrup. **Pickled ginger** (see page 12) is the Japanese condiment for sushi. It is easily recognised by its pink colour, it is available in jars.

GREEK-STYLE YOGHURT Made from cow's or ewe's milk and is especially rich, creamy and flavourful. Use thick whole milk yoghurt as an alternative.

HAZELNUTS
To skin hazelnuts, spread in a single layer on a roasting tin and bake in a preheated 180°C (350°F) Gas 4 oven until nutty, 10 minutes. Wrap the warm nuts in a coarse-textured cloth and rub briskly to loosen the skin as much as possible.

HERBS Always fresh, unless otherwise specified.

HOISIN SAUCE Slightly sweet, thick, dark brown sauce made from soy beans, garlic, and spices. Keeps indefinitely in a covered jar.

LEMON CURD Best home made. Follow the method for making passion curd (see page 127), but use 150ml (5floz) lemon juice and 1tsp grated lemon zest instead of the passion fruit and lemon juice mixture.

LEMON GRASS Long, grass-like herb with a strong citrus flavour and aroma. Use only the tender inner stalk as the outer leaves are tough. Use a mixture of grated lime and lemon zest as an alternative.

MANGO To slice or dice a fresh mango, find where the flat side of the stone is by rolling the mango on a work surface; it will settle on a flat side. Cut the peeled mango lengthwise on both sides of the stone so the knife just misses the stone. Put each mango piece cut side down and cut it lengthwise into slices,dice if required

MASA HARINA Finely ground corn flour used to make corn tortillas; available mail order and in speciality stores.

MIRIN Japanese rice wine, sweeter than sake and used only for cooking. Use medium dry sherry as an alternative.

MUSHROOMS To clean mushrooms, never wash in water but wipe clean with damp kitchen paper. **Field mushrooms** have an open, flat cap with exposed brown gills and a strong, savoury flavour. **Shiitake mushrooms** are an oriental variety with a powerful meaty flavour. There are many varieties of **wild mushrooms**; our favourites are chanterelles, cepes (also called porcini) and morels. Field or shiitake mushrooms can be used as an alternative.

MUSTARD (see page 13). We prefer French Dijon mustard; **grainy mustard** is made from crushed and ground mustard seeds, while the mustard seeds are ground completely smooth in **creamy mustard. Dried mustard** is one of the strongest and hottest of mustards.

NORI Sold in paper thin sheets. It is an edible seaweed that is a popular flavouring and garnish in Japanese cooking.

ONIONS When called for in the book, an onion is a yellow onion. A **medium red onion** weighs about 90g (3oz). A **Spanish onion** is a large, mild yellow onion. When we ask for a **spring onion**, we mean both the green and white parts, unless otherwise specified. A **shallot** has a more subtle flavour than a yellow onion.

OYSTERS Ask your fishmonger to shuck the oysters for you; cover and refrigerate for up to 2 days. Smoked oysters are available in tins.

PANCETTA Flavourful Italian streaky bacon. Store wrapped in the refrigerator for up to 3 weeks. Use streaky bacon as an alternative.

PARSLEY We use flat leaf parsley in all recipes.

PASSION FRUIT Choose wrinkled passion fruit as they are riper and therefore more sweet and juicy.

PLUM SAUCE Spicy, sweet, Chinese dipping sauce made from plums, chillies, vinegar, spices and sugar. It keeps indefinitely at room temperature in a covered jar.

POLENTA Made from ground corn, but is slightly coarser in texture and more golden in colour than medium cornmeal. Use coarse cornmeal as an alternative.

POMEGRANATE Only in season during the winter months. Choose fruits with a bright yellow skin streaked with bright pink. Store in the refrigerator for up to 3 weeks.

PRAWNS (see page 11). To devein raw prawns, cut off the head and peel away the shells and legs. With a sharp knife, cut along the top of each prawn and pull out the black vein. Wash and dry well.

PROSCIUTTO (see page 10) Italian raw ham that has been seasoned, salt-cured and air-dried.

RICE PAPERS Dried brittle translucent sheets made from rice flour. Available from Asian stores, they keep indefinitely.

ROCKET Long leaves and a peppery flavour. It is very perishable. Store tightly in a plastic bag in the refrigerator for up to 2 days. Leaves can be extremely gritty. Remove root ends and wash throughly in cold water just before using.

SAFFRON The world's most expensive spice. Choose saffron threads rather than safron powder.

SALT Always use sea salt, whether coarse or fine.

SAKE Japan's famous rice wine is widely used as a flavouring in Japanese sauces and marinades. Use dry sherry as an alternative.

SCALLOPS Queen scallops (see page 11) are about 1cm (½ in) across. **Sea scallops** (see page 11) are larger but vary in size. For canapés, choose sea scallops about 5cm (2in) across.

SESAME OIL We use Asian brands of sesame oil that are extracted from toasted sesame seeds. A lighter oil with a less intense flavour is also sold in healthfood stores. Sesame seeds are widely used as a flavouring in Chinese and Japanese cooking.

SHALLOT see onion.

SOBA NOODLES Very fine Japanese buckwheat noodles (see page156).

SOY SAUCE Major seasoning in Asian cooking and is available in a number of varieties ranging in colour and flavour. We use **light soy sauce** when we wish to preserve the colour of the food but **dark soy sauce** has a richer flavour. **Japanese soy sauce** called **shoyu** is sweeter, lighter and less salty; use light soy sauce as an alternative.

SUGAR Any white sugar (whether caster or granulated) that you have on hand.

SUGARCANE Available fresh, frozen and tinned, at Asian and Caribbean stores. When buying tinned, read the label to be sure the tins contain sugarcane sticks and not chopped sugarcane.

TAHINI Paste made from grinding roasted sesame seeds and is sold in jars in large supermarkets and Middle Eastern stores. Shake well before using.

TOMATO Fresh tomatoes are round or plum but always red and ripe. Leave unripe tomatoes to ripen on a window sill for a few days. **Tinned tomatoes** are peeled, chopped plum tomatoes. **Tomato passata** is plum tomatoes sieved completely smooth and is available in tins, jars and cartons. **Tomato purée** is concentrated cooked tomatoes, available in tins or tubes. **Sundried tomatoes** are marinated in oil in jars; drain before using.

VEGETABLES Washed and, unless otherwise stated, peeled in all recipes.

VINEGAR Red wine vinegar and **white wine vinegar** have different flavours and levels of acidity and should not be used interchangeably. **Balsamic vinegar** (see page 12) is dark in colour with a sweet, pungent flavour. Use red wine vinegar sweetened with a pinch of sugar as an alternative. **Rice vinegar** with its subtly sweet, mellow flavour is used extensively in Japanese cooking. White wine vinegar sweetened with a pinch of sugar can be used as an alternative in most recipes but not for flavouring sushi rice. In this case no substitution should be made.

WASABI Pungent green horseradish used in Japanese cuisine. It is available in a dried powdered form in tins and as a paste in tubes.

INDEX

AUTHORS' ACKNOWLEDGMENTS

We would like to thank:
Three very special **Books for Cooks** cooks for their generosity and expertise. Kim Barber for her indispensible sushi masterclass and for letting us include her fabulous Sushi Rice Balls in the book. Jennifer Joyce for lending us her Southwestern and Pacific hors d'oeuvres recipes. Ursula Ferrigno for allowing us to minitaturise her Red Onion Schiaciatta and Aubergine Polpette.
Heidi Lascelles, founder and proprietor of Books for Cooks, for supporting us in all our ventures, whether writing books, teaching classes, moving house or having a baby.
Juliet Kindersley, for a mother's love, care and understanding. And for the loan of her kitchen, in which many of the recipes were tried and tested.
James Middlehurst, for giving us the green light.
Baby Frances, for letting us borrow her mummy. Her mummy Julia Pemberton Hellums for being just great, again.

And most of all, Stuart Jackman. For giving us a chance.
For making it happen.

MAIL ORDER SOURCES

FORTNUM & MASON
181 Piccadilly
London W1A 1ER
0171-734-8040
www.fortnumandmason.com
Catalogue available. Gourmet groceries and an extensive range of ready-made canapé bases and cases, including chocolate cups.

HARVEY NICHOLS
109-125 Knightsbridge
London SW1X 7RJ
0171-235-5000
Delivery service. Luxury foods and speciality ingredients from around the world.

THE SPICE SHOP
1 Blenheim Crescent
London W11 2EE
0171-221-4448
Catalogue available. Spices and ethnic ingredients, including mini poppadoms and chipotles in adobo.

COOL CHILE COMPANY
PO Box 5702
London W11 2GS
0870-9021145
Catalogue available. Dried chillies and Southwestern speciality ingredients.

DIVERTIMENTI MAIL ORDER LIMITED
PO Box 6611
London SW15 2WG
0181-246-4300
Catalogue available. Kitchenware, tableware and gourmet ingredients.